Tears of the Levant

tales from Syria and Iraq (2012 to 2017)

By Carsten Stormer

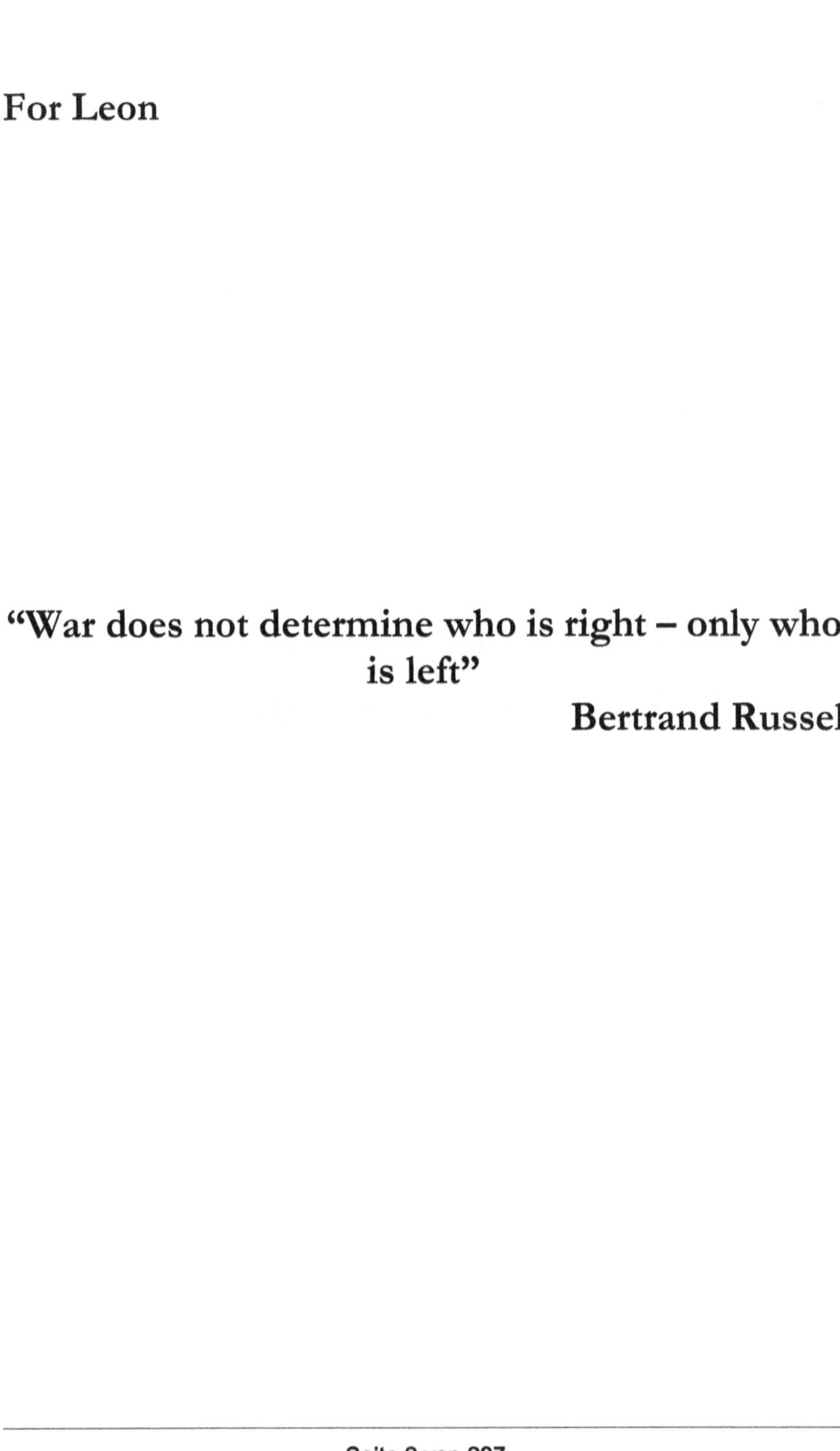

For Leon

"War does not determine who is right – only who
is left"

Bertrand Russel

In spring of 2011 a group of boys in the southern Syrian city of Daraa, inspired by the civilian uprisings in Tunisia and Egypt, grabbed their spry cans and wrote some graffitis on walls.

'Freedom. Down with the regime. Your turn, Doctor'

Within days, security forces stormed their homes and detained the boys and tortured them.

The teenagers' detention prompted a wave of angry protests demanding their release, in what many refer to as the spark to Syria's nationwide uprising – which soon turned into civil war and eventually into the most brutal war and biggest human catastrophe of modern times.

Since then, between 367,965 and 560,000 are believed to have been killed.

Six million Syrians have been internally displaced within Syria. Five millions living as refugees outside of Syria.

Chapter 1: Lebanon, March 2012

From my seat in the plane, a Boeing of the Lebanese airline MEA, I gazed out of the window at the crowded streets of Beirut far below. As the plane prepared to land I couldn't help wondering whether I was making a huge mistake. In my luggage were a bullet-proof jacket, a couple of cameras and a military helmet; and in my head was the crazy idea that I was somehow going to bluff my way over the border into Syria. My goal was the beleaguered city of Homs, focal point of the rebellion against the Syrian regime. For weeks the city had been dominating the headlines in the world press: whole districts of the city were being encircled by the Syrian army, inhabitants were being starved into submission, demonstrators were being shot dead by army marksmen. Only a few weeks earlier the well-known American reporter Marie Colvin had been killed along with French photographer Remi Ochlik when the house in which they had been staying was shelled by the Syrian army. All these impressions were seething wildly inside my head. I was fired up and determined; but more than anything I was afraid.

My plan was quite simple. It was still technically possible to travel to Damascus from the Lebanon; visas were supposed to be available at the frontier. On the other hand, foreign journalists were certainly not likely to be welcomed. For this reason, I had made up a story on the strength of which I hoped to convince the border guards to let me through. I would present myself as a Christian pilgrim interested in visiting churches, monasteries and holy sites in the ancient land of St Paul and St Simeon: the Ananias chapel in Damascus, the St Thekla monastery in Maalula, the cathedral in Homs, St Simeon's citadel near Aleppo. Once inside Syria I hoped to be able to make my way by bus and taxi to the war zone in Homs. At a souvenir shop in Beirut I bought myself a plastic rosary and thus my ruse was complete, in theory at least. Two days later I was heading for the Lebanese-Syrian border in a taxi with my cameras concealed under the front seats. And from then on everything started to go pear-shaped.

The frontier post was in chaos. Thousands of people were jostling against the barrier, waving their passports in the air. Syrian families, often of several generations, were gesticulating wildly as they argued with the Lebanese border guards and begged to be allowed through. A huge queue of vehicles stretched back as far as the eye could see: cars and minibuses laden with human beings and all their worldly goods, mattresses, fridges, televisions, bits of furniture, everything that might be needed for a life on the run. Syrians were fleeing their country as sailors desert their sinking ship. All of them had one simple goal: to get out of Syria as fast as possible.

And there was I, equally desperate to get in.

The counters at the Syrian check post were all manned by uniformed officials, yet nobody was queueing at any of them. I showed my passport, spouted my little story – and instantly realised it was not going to wash. But instead of returning my passport to me and waving me back into the Lebanon the border guards, amiable but insistent, escorted me to the office of a functionary from the Syrian intelligence service. There were already a few other folks, clearly all journalists with made up agendas. I remained sitting there, grinning foolishly at the intelligence officer, who ordered tea for us. Without beating about the bush he explained that he did not believe either of our stories and that, much though it pained him to say so, there was no way we would be permitted to enter Syria. He said that in recent months far too many foreign journalists had been making their way illegally into Syria in order to propagate evil lies about the country and the Assad regime. We nodded, took a sip of tea and asked politely if we could have our passports back. All right, all in good time, his people were just going through the details in the passports; if these tallied with what we had said, we would be free to go.

It was at that moment that I began to get worried. The rubber stamps in my passport clearly indicated that I was no pilgrim. Just then the electricity supply went dead. We waited, drank tea, waited some more, were given some more tea. Still the electricity was off. Eventually the intelligence officer barked out an order, a subordinate appeared, some whispering went on, the subordinate went out again and soon came back with our passports. After making a note of the passport numbers he told us we could go.

Clearly Plan A had not worked. So instead I decided to go to Tripoli in northern Lebanon and research a piece about refugees. The main centre for Syrian refugees in Lebanon was the northern city of. In the various hospitals of the city lay many war victims, all of whom spoke of massacres carried out by Syrian government forces against the civilian population. They mentioned snipers shooting indiscriminately at anyone stepping out of a house; sustained bombardment of residential areas; demonstrators being summarily executed in the street; corpses left to rot in the roadway as a deterrent. Most of these refugees chose to remain anonymous, as even in the Lebanon they feared the long arm of the Assad regime. They said opposition figures and refugees had in recent months often been picked up by Syrian and Lebanese secret agents and sent back to Syria.

They all told different versions of the same story. Men and women, old people and young children, almost all of them Sunnis, they had been caught up in the Arabian Spring, which had dragged on into a second year and mutated into civil war in Syria.

I arrived in Tripoli on a cold, rainy morning in March. A contact took me around all the hospitals where victims of the Syrian war were being treated. It was

then, in the corridors and wards of hospitals reeking
of pus, burned flesh and disinfectants, that a window
opened for me and for the first time I got a real
glimpse of the civil war in Syria.

When the final screw had been driven into the
patient's foot, the bullet wound had been dressed and
the man with the jagged wound in his thigh had
stopped screaming, Dr Ahmed stood exhausted in
the linoleum covered corridor of the hospital,
between side rooms full of seriously wounded people,
and debated which patient he should treat next. In
Room 532 lay 13-year old Ghafran Koukaz, whose
first name meant mercy. A sniper had aimed at her
from his hiding place and shot a bullet through her
thigh, severing the nerves and reducing her leg to a
lump of unfeeling flesh. Next door in Room 533 was
Hassan, 22 years old, who had trodden on a landmine
whilst trying to flee from Syria. The explosion had
ripped both his hands off and shards of shrapnel
were still lodged in his ravaged face. Dr Ahmed's
eyes came to rest on Room 532: the little girl must
come first.

A pink teddy bear stood on the bedside table,
surrounded by packets of pills. Ghafran was sleeping
while her mother kept watch at her side. Dr Ahmed
stroked Ghafran's hair; there was little else he could
do.

At that time Dr Ahmed had 37 Syrian wound
victims in his charge. The hospital where he worked

was on the outskirts of Tripoli, surrounded by half-finished blocks of flats and roads studded with potholes. A large, heavily built man in a diamond pattern pullover, 40 years of age, he had rings of fatigue under his eyes and the neon ceiling lights made his skin look yellowish, almost like desiccated cheese. He had had no sleep for days on end, nothing more than the odd couple of hours dozing at a patient's bedside. Sometimes he would sleep in an overcrowded flat belonging to a friend, sharing the space with a dozen other refugees. Always with him was his stock of worldly belongings: two carrier bags containing a change of clothes.

For he too was a Syrian, who had fled to the Lebanon from his home city of Homs in early March 2012. He had been one of thirty doctors on the rebel side who had stayed behind in Homs: there, in the secrecy of private apartments serving as field hospitals, he and his colleagues had tried to give emergency treatment to the collateral victims of the Syrian revolution: children with head trauma, women with gaping wounds in their torso, fighters of the Free Syrian Army (FSA). There had been six mobile teams each consisting of five doctors, and they had operated in different parts of the city, burrowing like moles from one building to the next through holes in shattered masonry.

Dr Ahmed sat down on a well-worn bench provided for visitors, a cup of golden brown tea in his trembling fingers, and in his soft voice described what he had experienced in Syria.

Initially, when Syrians were just starting to come out into the streets to demonstrate against the Assad regime, Dr Ahmed was still working as a surgeon at a government hospital in Homs. "More and more wounded people were coming to the hospital each day. Quite a few were arrested while they were in the theatre undergoing an operation." That included demonstrators, members of opposition factions and rebels. Some of his colleagues, Dr Ahmed said, deliberately ended the lives of certain patients. Then one day, air force intelligence officers came to arrest a man with a gaping abdominal wound while Dr Ahmed was operating on him. "Don't worry," one of the men said, "we'll stitch him up for you." The following day that patient's corpse was found stretched out in front of his family home. That was the moment when Dr Ahmed decided to join the rebels. He placed his family members in hiding with friends and slipped into the underworld.

As the electricity supply was frequently disrupted and the doctors faced a chronic shortage of medicines, anaesthetics, respirators and surgical implements, many lives could not be saved. The makeshift hospital, located in an apartment in the Baba Amr district of the city, was frequently shelled, so patients had to be moved into neighbouring flats for safety. Often there was nothing the doctors could do except watch helplessly while wounded people died in front of them. "But we were able to save a lot of them," declared Dr Ahmed, a faint smile stealing over his exhausted face. At the end of February, when the bombardment became too heavy to bear, he quit Baba Amr, taking with him twelve wounded men of whom three were in a comatose state. The flight to Lebanon took two days. The group travelled by night; during the daytime they came under shellfire and had to hide in ditches and among the crops in fields. Of the twelve wounded only four survived the journey.

Now, in the relative safety of the Lebanon, he was helping out as best he could. Up on the fifth floor of the hospital he kept busy changing dressings, setting fractures, carrying out operations, amputating limbs, all the time inwardly yearning for mental relief and a sense of purpose. He felt he was serving the revolution – and he was drowning his helplessness in hard work. The Lebanese doctors were quietly supportive.

The Lebanese government was in a predicament. On the one hand it had a pact with Syria and had to tell Syrian deserters they were not allowed to settle in the Lebanon; on the other hand, it was unwilling to anger its other Arab neighbours by sending refugees back into Syria. Any Syrian who managed to get into the Lebanon was treated as a visitor, not a refugee, and allowed six months' leave to remain; in this way the Lebanese government contrived to preserve its humanitarian credentials while avoiding a diplomatic rift. Syrian activists inside the Lebanon reckoned that some 20,000 Syrian refugees had already crossed into the country; more were arriving every day. Even so the Lebanese Red Cross did not appear to see the need to take action. Hundreds of people queued at the border crossings each day for a visitor's permit. Others, if they were lucky enough not to fall foul of land mines, frontier guards or army patrols on the way, entered the Lebanon clandestinely with the help of activists or members of the Syrian Free Army. Everyone was heading in the same direction: out.

Their legal status still ambiguous, the refugees took shelter in apartments made available by the network of activists, in schools, or in slums on the edge of the city. There could be as many as thirty people to as many square metres, more and more families being squeezed into each flat. Living space was at a premium, rents were rocketing. Seats on the Lebanese lifeboat were running out. Life revolved around the gathering of news and rumours. Were fresh battles taking place? New Syrian offensives? How were the family members back home, were they still alive? Life had turned into a vacuum in which time no longer existed.

It was on the first anniversary of the Syrian revolution that I visited him a second time: Dr

Ahmed, the doctor who guarded his plastic bag of worldly belongings as if it was made of gold. Rain was relentlessly battering the window panes of the hospital in Tripoli, and the water was flowing down the glass in rivulets. The fugitive Syrian doctor was sitting on a folding chair next to a patient's bed, his eyes closed. He had fallen asleep with his head lolling on his chest. All around was restless activity. Men with amputated limbs, some with steel attachments sticking out, were preparing posters to celebrate the anniversary. A television team from Al Jazeera was expected: they were going to film the ceremonies. It was a Friday. Like their fellow countrymen in Syria these patients wanted to mount a demonstration. We were invited to celebrate the anniversary alongside the wounded refugees. Men with stumps of limbs offered us chilled cola in plastic cups; patients in plaster casts were exchanging cigarettes. Roast chicken, chips and hummus were on the menu.

Among the people celebrating was Abu Jaman. For eleven months he had dreamed of a free Syria; then one day he had woken up to find himself in the operation theatre of this hospital in Lebanon. He was 36 years old and had an emaciated face and a wild beard; he was following the goings on in the ward with glittering eyes. Over his shoulders was draped a shawl with the colours of the revolution – green, white and black with three white stars. His left arm had been amputated above the elbow and was enveloped in a grimy bandage; splinters of metal from a shell were still lodged in his chest and abdomen. In the next bed lay his comrade in arms, Muhammad, 32 years old. His right leg had been cut off above the knee and down his left leg an ugly scar ran from the groin to the calf. Abu Jaman had a cigarette between his lips, even though the ward sister had declared that smoking was forbidden The way the patients viewed things Ward 5 was a liberated zone, part of the revolution, and a nurse had no jurisdiction in it.

An orderly barged into the ward, wrinkled his nose at the cigarette smoke and announced that it was time for people's dressings to be changed. But Abu Jaman sent him packing. Get out of here, that can wait, we're busy doing things for the revolution. Then he pulled his scraggy beard with the fingers of his remaining hand. "I'd love to teach that fellow a lesson," he said with a grin, wagging the stump of his other arm. "But sadly that's no longer possible."

Abu Jaman was merely a pawn in a great game of chess, where it was uncertain which player would win. Under a hail of fire, he had dragged the dead and wounded to the rebels' field hospital, he said. Just when he was about to rescue a girl a shell had burst close by; a shard of shrapnel had sliced his arm off and the child had been killed. He didn't consider it a big deal that he had lost an arm: that was his contribution to the revolution, or so he tried to convince himself. This was the defence mechanism of a traumatized person which let him blot out reality and make the present bearable while clinging to the hope that his sacrifice had not been in vain, since he knew full well that his life would never be the same again. "But I feel very bad about not having saved that little girl," he said. "I think of her every day." And he lit another cigarette from the butt of the old one.

At seven in the evening the festivities began, marking the anniversary of the revolution. There was a march past of disabled fighters, holding up placards, waving the Syrian flag and shouting slogans. "Down with Assad! Freedom for Syria! *Allahu akbar! Allahu akbar!*" Young men, holding a catheter in one hand and dragging the stand on which their drip bag was mounted with the other, tottered from ward to ward directing operations and gesticulating. Others were holding up the ones who could not walk unaided, pushing wheelchairs, leading blind men along. Some visitors had brought a cake with "God damn your soul, Assad" written on it in icing. Motionless clouds of grey smoke from countless cigarettes hung in mid-air like an early morning mist. The men sang and clapped their hands until their voices got hoarse and their hands burned, creating a curtain of sound which resounded from the walls of the ward. The throng became ever more drunk with euphoria and fury while the Al Jazeera team filmed them. At some point Dr Ahmed was woken by the noise. He was too tired to clap, but a gentle smile played on his lips.

"Freedom for Syria!" he murmured, making the Victory sign.

Chapter 2: Tripoli – northern Lebanon

While I was in Tripoli interviewing Syrian refugees the conflict in Syria spread right into the capital, Damascus. Shelling of the rebel strongholds of Homs and Idlib was continuing, and Saudi Arabia was supplying the rebels with weapons. The organization Human Rights Watch accused both sides of torturing prisoners and executing them. The revolution had lost its innocence.

The war in Syria was splitting Lebanese society down the middle: into those who supported the Syrian president and those who opposed him. Already resting on shaky foundations, the Lebanese state was being hollowed out by the ever increasing, endless flow of refugees. Street fights between Sunnis and Shiites were beginning to break out in Tripoli.

In a gloomy teashop on the coastal hillside of Tripoli I met Feiras Abo Oday, a 26-year old refugee who seemed to have run up against a dead end in Tripoli. A chilly wind was blowing into the cafe from the Mediterranean Sea below. Feiras was ready to talk but his voice kept failing him. Hunched up like a tortoise, he was sitting bent over a rickety table and inhaling the smoke from his cigarette deep into his lungs. Tears were pouring down his face and with one hand he sketched a movement as if trying to wipe away his memories like a speck of dirt. Since fleeing Syria he had been working in this teashop, which was owned by a Syrian acquaintance of his. Just now there was only one customer, sucking a shisha pipe. The rain had chased all the strollers on the promenade back into their homes. The Mediterranean was crashing against the coastal highway, beating its elemental rhythm. Feiras was unwilling to reveal his real name as he was afraid: afraid of Syrian agents, of informants, of the Lebanese secret service. He was a broken youth with scars on his body and burn marks on his soul. While his eyes roamed nervously from side to side and his fingers clung tightly to the edge of the wooden table, under the flickering neon light, he told me his story.

Oday served as a conscript in the Syrian army for a period of twenty-two months. It was in the fifteenth month of his service that his countrymen, all over Syria, began their demonstrations. Oday was posted at a road block in Dara'a, the city in southern Syria where the revolution started. "Our officers told us to shoot terrorists. But I couldn't see any terrorists, only people demonstrating." He was obviously still deeply upset when recalling these things. His sergeant had shot an old man; one of his companions was put to death for refusing to shoot a demonstrator; a deserter was executed. Oday resolved to cross over and join the Free Syrian Army as so many others had already done; but he didn't know how to do it. "I wasn't afraid of dying. But I hadn't got the money to buy myself a Kalashnikov." He assured me he had never shot at demonstrators, only into the air or at walls.

Refusal to obey orders is how the army describes such dereliction. In July 2011 he was sent to the infamous Sydnaia military prison outside Damascus. He was one of thirty prisoners confined in a space measuring thirty square metres, blindfolded, lying face down on the ground with their wrists chained to their ankles. The youngest prisoner was a mere thirteen years old. This went on hour after hour, for days, the only interruptions being for questioning and torture. "I was forced naked into a car tyre, hung up from the ceiling and beaten with sticks and cables until I could no longer feel anything in my arms or legs," he said, his features hardening like the scab on a wound. That type of torture was known as *dulab*, the tyre. Oday started weeping again, then wiped his face and drew a deep breath. "I wasn't even able to put my clothes back on without help." After sixteen days he was told to sign a paper exonerating all those who had tortured him. The document stated that he had undergone no ill treatment while in prison and that he promised to report any colleague of his who failed to shoot demonstrators. He was then released, and returned to his unit. His period of military service came to an end in October 2011; in November he fled to the Lebanon for fear that he might be conscripted again. It cost him four hundred dollars to bribe a border official to give him an exit visa.

In my travels through Lebanon I kept meeting Syrian refugees who offered to smuggle me into their country. Homs? No problem, it's just around the corner, a little hop over the border. Aleppo? Sure, just say when you want to go. It was as if they were proposing a holiday excursion. I hesitated. What, enter a war zone with total strangers? Illegally, without any safeguards? My gut said yes, my head objected. I decided to follow my head. I wasn't prepared to risk my life so lightly. The stories I had heard in the last few days had unnerved me. Like the story told by two injured FSA fighters I met in a safe house in a small village. From their window one got a lovely view of the gentle hills which separate the Lebanon from Syria.

Younis Abu Salimar, 27, and Muhammad Abu Uday, 19, claimed they were not afraid to die. These two FSA fighters were in hiding, recovering from their wounds. They refused to give their real names and kept their faces covered with drapery. Armed activists from the opposition movement were outside, guarding the approach to their living quarters, and two cars with armed men sitting in the back were blocking the road. Before we could advance along the road and enter the house my Syrian interpreter and I were frisked and our pockets were searched for weapons. That was how deep fear and suspicion ran.

Muhammad had lost his left hand during the fighting in Baba Amr in February. The stump of his wrist projected from the sleeve of his black pullover.

Buried in his thigh were pieces of shrapnel from a shell which had burst beside him. Younis had joined the rebels after being arrested by army intelligence men in June 2011 for taking part in a demonstration against the Assad regime. He had been tortured in prison for six weeks, he said, pulling up the legs of his tracksuit to show the poorly healed wounds on his calves and feet. "This is where they punctured my leg with a drill." The scars on his forearms and hands, he explained, had been inflicted by burning cigarettes and electric probes. "They also cut off one of my testicles." Younis was limping badly and had to be supported by his friend Muhammad when moving about.

For the time being the revolution was carrying on without the two fighters. Their greatest enemy was time. Day and night they kept scanning for news of Syria, flicking through television channels, using their mobile phones, poring over Facebook and fuzzy YouTube footage. The war, friends, colleagues and family all seemed far away; now, as illegal migrants, these fighters had become mere spectators of the rebellion. So they were keen to get back into Syria as soon as possible and rejoin their comrades in their rebel units, eager to fight and take revenge against the shadowy Shabiha brigades and against the Alawi faction, including Assad himself, which they held responsible for all the slaughter. Bitter events had sunk deep into their psyche like a time capsule buried in soil, an indelible relic of horror.

Border controls on either side of the frontier had been intensified during the past months in response to the deluge of Syrians crossing the soft frontier illegally in order to escape from the fighting in their homeland. Soldiers were now patrolling day and night. Land mines, armoured vehicles, night vision scanners were making it difficult for refugees to get out of Syria and for fixers to smuggle things in: arms, food, medicines, journalists. Yet the tide of refugees could not be stemmed. Day by day more people crossed over the line and many of them gathered in Wadi Khalad, a green valley surrounded by mountains whose peaks were sprinkled with snow like icing sugar on a Christmas cake. Road blocks set up by the Lebanese army prevented reporters from accessing the refugees. "This is a simple security precaution," explained a border guard after a lengthy study of our passports "It's to stop armed rebels from slipping into our country." A Syrian refugee who was sitting next to me in the car had forgotten some of his papers and was terrified of being arrested and sent back into Syria. Beads of sweat were on his brow and his lips were trembling. "I've had it," he moaned. For three quarters of an hour the border guards searched the vehicle, examined documents, noted down passport numbers: then they let us go. They warned my Syrian companion that he must remember to have his visa ready for inspection next time. Then we tried to get to the borderland refugees by a different route.

At the border post of Kaa, in the Bekaa valley in north east Lebanon, a frontier guard once again eyed our passports dubiously, took down details, asked questions. "Just for the sake of security," he assured us with a smile. He let us through. "This is a dangerous spot. Fighting was going on all along the border earlier today. The Syrian army shelled villages close to the border." Dozens of buses and lorries crammed full of people and baggage were waiting at the checkpoint, eager to get out of Syria. In the distance we could hear the explosions and shots of a battle.

We were now in a no man's land between Syria and the Lebanon. About a hundred families had taken refuge there, among the ruins of abandoned farmhouses and donkey sheds. In the small town of Arsal, close to the frontier, about 256 refugee Syrian families were living together with their Lebanese hosts, about 1500 people in all. A truck pulled up in front of a dirty hovel in which thirty-two refugees were sharing three tiny rooms. There were fourteen more people, women and children, in the back of the lorry: new arrivals. The driver, a farmer from Arsal, had picked them up where they crossed the border illegally into Lebanon. The women were crying and the children wailing, their small bodies shivering uncontrollably. There they stood like a herd of frightened sheep. "We ran away from Homs one afternoon. On our way we were shelled and shot at by snipers. Why would they want to kill us?" asked one woman, throwing her hands in the air. "God be praised!" Somewhere nearby someone let off a firework. The children threw themselves to the ground and sought refuge among their mothers' skirts, eyes wide with fear, a suppressed cry on their lips.

We could not stay long in Arsal. The mayor warned us that the area was under the control of Hezbollah, the Lebanese Shiite militia, which was on President Assad's side. He asked us to leave as quickly as possible – our presence could make problems for the refugees, and indeed for himself. He apologized, asked us to forgive him, invited us to lunch with him. Afterwards we drove quickly back to Tripoli.

It was my last day in Tripoli. I wanted to touch base with some refugees I'd met earlier, relatives of my constant companion in recent days, a Syrian activist who had fled Homs months before.

This is it, I thought, my final interview. Abu Shadi, my guide, had been working tirelessly for me, interpreting, making appointments, persuading people to be interviewed, and by way of thanks I decided to invite him out for a meal. But Abu Shadi shook his head and said that according to the rules of Syrian hospitality a guest must never be allowed to pay. He seemed to forget that he himself was a guest in another country. Instead he asked whether I minded going somewhere out of the way. The night before two children in poor shape had been admitted to a certain hospital. My stomach was grumbling, I had a headache and I was dog tired. I had already collected enough material for my project; did I really need those two children? But I didn't wish to be rude or hurt the feelings of my loyal companion, so I said yes, sure, let's go and see them.

Chapter 3: Ahmad and Hanadi

I had no idea that the decision to visit that hospital would change the direction of my life. The visit was going to shape my personal attitude and my professional approach for years to come.

We took the lift to reach the top floor of the Hôpital de la Paix, which is where the burns unit was located. I could guess the kind of scene which awaited me, but there was no pulling back now. We entered a room with a view over the sea and I saw her: Hanadi Abba, a thirteen-year-old girl, lying there scarcely able to breathe. Burns covered 85% of her body, her skin had erupted in blisters and a bright red secretion was oozing out through her bandages. She was staring vacantly, her eyes blank, her mouth an expressionless line. Her body was twitching and she was groaning with pain, a pain that not even morphine and other drugs had been enough to dispel. Standing there in front of her I could see little more than a mass of burned skin and raw flesh. Hanadi Abba looked at me but I couldn't tell whether she was aware of my presence. Then she closed her eyes as if signalling that she wanted me to go. In the next room lay her brother Ahmad, aged seventeen. 75% of his body had been ravaged by fire. His half closed eyes were visible through the gauze mask covering his face. He raised an arm as if he wanted to say something, but no sound came from his lips. Then he let his arm fall and turned his head away to one side.

The sight of these two moribund children hit me like a punch in the stomach and took my breath away. I felt ashamed to be standing there, up on the top floor with a grand view of Tripoli and the Mediterranean. I was supposed to take photographs but I couldn't bring myself to do it. Shame, shock, anger; I didn't know what to feel.

All I knew was that I had no business there. I had seen similar cases in Afghanistan, Somalia and Iraq and knew that nobody could survive such burns. Standing before those two fatally injured children I felt furious with Abu Shadi. Why had he brought me there? What the hell was I supposed to do, apart from standing around, taking photographs and feeling like a vulture eyeing a piece of carrion? Here were two young people whose lives were ending before they had properly started, thanks to being sucked into the whirlpool of the Arabian Spring.

A young man with an earnest look in his eyes came up to me, shook my hand and introduced himself. His name was Amin and he was a cousin of the young patients. He briefly explained what had happened. Hanadi and Ahmad were from Homs. On 13th May 2012 they had been in the kitchen of the flat where they lived with their parents when a shell came in. The gas cooker had exploded and brother and sister had been enveloped in a ball of fire. No hospital in war torn Homs could take them in, so some FSA fighters had smuggled them out of the city, moving by night through the maze of back streets, avoiding army road blocks and loyalist militias, and driven them to the mine studded frontier thirty kilometres away. Their parents had stayed behind as they had two other children to worry about. Workers of the International Red Cross had met them in Lebanon and taken them to the Hôpital de la Paix in Tripoli. Now Amin stood in front of me with arms hanging down and a dazed expression. "Can you help?" he asked, and a flicker of hope could be seen in his eyes, together with a silent demand for me to do something.

What I would really have liked to do was turn around and run away. But instead I went downstairs again and knocked on the door of the doctor in chief. Gabriel al-Sabah, white haired and jaded, dark rings of fatigue under his eyes, was sitting at his desk wondering how he was going to treat all those Syrian patients with very severe injuries and no money who had been delivered to his hospital. And now here was a bothersome Western journalist. He eyed me and gestured silently to an empty chair in front of his desk. "It's a miracle that those two survived," he said in answer to my question. "The dangerous journey from Homs to the Lebanon could easily have killed them. But yes, it is possible that they could be saved." A skin transplant would at least prolong their lives. However, their bodies had been so badly burned there wasn't enough skin left for the transplant. "We would need skin from a laboratory, and that is something very expensive which can only be obtained abroad, in America or Germany. We could do the operation here in the Lebanon, only we would need skin cultures from abroad." As he sat there in his office al-Sabah's voice betrayed anger and despair at his own helplessness. Either the skin would have to be imported for the children or they would have to travel to where the skin was. Either way, time was running out fast.

I asked Dr al-Sabah for permission to photograph the child patients, and this sparked off a tirade about the media in general and reporters in particular. He said he had lived through all the Lebanese wars and seen how reporters were always involved, taking their photographs, publishing them, being paid for them, maybe even becoming famous for them, yet not bringing about any change for the people of Lebanon. One war had ended only for another to begin. The media circus had used Lebanon as its performing ring, and from it derived fame and glory for itself.

What could I say? The doctor was right. If I'd been in a pub, say, I might have launched into a debate about the power of the media, the responsibility to report things, the importance of giving a voice to those who were not being listened to. I would have referred to the holocaust, Ruanda, Srebrenica, mass rape in the Congo. But here, on the doorstep of a war, I felt I had no right to push my moral pretensions at someone who was fighting a losing battle of his own. I told the doctor I would try to help. I couldn't make any promises, but I would contact aid agencies, doctors, diplomats and friends and make a buzz on Facebook and Twitter. "At least that will be better than doing nothing," I opined. "Do whatever you think best," replied Dr al-Sabah, making a gesture which meant it was time for me to go. I could understand how he felt. In the course of a few weeks in Lebanon I had reached the limit of what I could bear; and the doctor was facing the same horrors day in and day out with no end in sight. How much could any man endure? Particularly a doctor who had vowed to help people and found he lacked the means to do so.

I went back up to the ward and took photographs of Hanadi and Ahmad. Then I asked Abu Shadi to take me to the nearest internet cafe. I uploaded the images onto Facebook and posted a short description of what had happened to them. I mentioned that they would both die if no help was forthcoming.

And then the miracle happened.

18th March 2012. My friend Veronika Faltenbacher was sitting on a sofa at home surfing the net, and she read my post on Facebook. She sent a text message to an acquaintance of hers who then alerted Dr Hubertus von Voss. Dr von Voss started looking for a suitable hospital. The following day an appeal was launched and circulated on the net. In under a week a six figure sum was raised. A donation came from a children's charity; another large sum was handed over by a well-known German publicist. The doctors at a specialist hospital in Munich gave the green light, saying they would treat the children provided their expenses were covered. The German ambassador to the United Nations Peter Wittig, who happened to be the brother-in-law of Dr Hubertus von Voss, then made good use of semi-official channels and his own diplomatic skills and persuaded his colleagues in Beirut to go through the necessary formalities and finalize travel arrangements for the two children, who had no passports or other papers with them. Very soon Hanadi and Ahmad, who had been put in a coma, were ready to be airlifted from Beirut to Munich on a chartered rescue flight.

Help had arrived just in the nick of time. Hanadi's wounds had become infected and she had to be given an oxygen mask before she could be moved. Luckily she was just fit for air transport. By the time the plane landed in Munich in the evening of 31st March several of her vital organs were failing and the doctors held out little hope for her. Over the course of several days fifteen different surgeons from the hospital performed a series of operations on both children, offering their services free of charge. At last it was certain that Hanadi and Ahmad would survive. They remained in an induced coma for eight weeks, until finally they woke up to find themselves in a foreign country surrounded by strangers, strangers who had given them a new lease of life.

The two children were probably the first Syrian refugees to enter Germany. They had to undergo a number of further operations and take medication to combat the pain and trauma, for their injuries had been exceedingly serious. But they quickly became integrated into German society and learned to speak German. Hanadi went to school, Ahmed became an apprentice in a commercial firm, sang in a refugee choir, and even shook hands with the German president Joachim Gauck. Meanwhile their cousin Amin got married to a German girl, had a child and trained as a master electrician. There is nobody I feel more proud of than these strong and admirable youngsters.

My contribution was minimal. If Abu Shadi hadn't insisted on making that unscheduled call at the burns unit I would never have met Ahmed and Hanadi. In the event I posted a few photos on the internet and that was it. If those images had not been circulated the two children would have died, no doubt about that. But the real miracle was performed by the doctors at the Munich hospital.

It was hardly to be believed that any story from Syria could end happily. That fateful day in Tripoli, 18th March 2012, transformed my life – at a personal level, as it created the invisible bond which links me to Hanadi and Ahmad; but also as a journalist. Thanks to a tiny incident I had been able to do a little more than report on all the horrors. Now whenever the world's sufferings make me sink down into cynicism I think of Hanadi, Ahmad and all the people who came forward to help them, not because they hoped for any gain but simply because it was the right thing to do at that moment. Four months later I finally made it into the rebel controlled areas in norther Syria. My goal was to reach the metropolis of Aleppo.

Chapter 4: Aleppo – summer 2012

Aleppo is the commercial hub of Syria. I visited it for the first time in July 2012. Rebels had been planning an assault on the city for weeks. During that time hundreds of fighters from all over the north had been sneaking into the city. In small groups of thirty or forty men, moving by night along village paths and back streets, avoiding Syrian army checkpoints and road blocks, they had infiltrated all quarters of the city and hidden in cellars and in the homes of activists and sympathizers. Their numbers grew day after day. Opposition elements in the capital city Damascus were keeping in constant contact with the rebels in the outlying provinces, supplying provisions, arranging accommodation and coordinating the distribution of munitions – brand new sniping rifles, Belgian assault guns, ammunition, image intensifiers, bazookas, uniforms. Out of sight of the Syrian army supplies for the freedom fighters were filtering into the rebel held districts of Aleppo, not in a torrent but in a quiet, steady flow gradually filling the backwaters of Aleppo.

One summer evening in the inner courtyard of a house in a suburb of Aleppo I watched men in camouflage assemble on parade. They had assault rifles slung over their shoulders and grenades dangling from their belts. I saw them laboriously compile an inventory of the stuff contained in some sacks: brand new sniping rifles, masses of ammunition, bazookas, Belgian assault rifles and dozens of image intensifiers still wrapped in plastic. They would not explain where all this gear had come from.

The commanding officer raised one of the night vision gadgets into the air and his men crowed with delight and started dancing about to cries of *"Allahu akbar! Allahu akbar!"* – God is great – as they brandished their Kalashnikovs above their heads. Then they put everything back into the jute sacks, tied them up and stowed them in the boots of various vehicles: cars, taxis and minibuses. They slipped off their battle gear and changed back into jeans and shirts. There were about thirty of them and they squeezed into the six or seven vehicles, then drove off under cover of night, choosing minor roads to avoid Syrian army checkpoints. Outriders on motorbikes went ahead spying out the land, checking for army roadblocks and using radio transmitters to keep in touch with the rest of the unit which followed a couple of kilometres to the rear. They were heading for Aleppo.

I was brought into Aleppo in the luggage compartment of a taxi. The city was still controlled by the Syrian regime, but an attack by the rebels was imminent. Supporters and opponents of the Assad regime were constantly vying for control of the city with its population of two million, and each street and each block belonged to either one or the other. There were plenty of Assad supporters in Aleppo, many of them rich businessmen who profited from the existing regime. Police and army checkpoints had been set up all over the city and the streets were patrolled by the dreaded Shabiha militia. The rebels drove me hither and thither from one hiding place to the next, making long detours and switching vehicles several times.

Opposition members, in the privacy of flats belonging to rebels and opponents of the government, were at that time busily preparing for the overthrow of the regime. Up until July 2012 Aleppo had for the most part been spared from open conflict, though in certain areas such as the Salaheddine district there had been mass demonstrations and daily clashes between government supporters and their opponents. The group I met on the roof terrace of a nondescript block of flats next to a main road in Salaheddine consisted of a bizarre assortment of lawyers, journalists, students, shopkeepers and rebels. These people assembled there only at night and in strictest secrecy. They used to sleep by day and devote their nights to the revolution. Most of them were wanted by the police or had their names on the intelligence service hit list; they could never stay in the same place for more than a few hours and had to keep well away from their own homes in order not to put their families in danger. They used to sleep somewhere different each night.

"We will soon have liberated Aleppo," bragged Abdul Hamid, a 36-year old lawyer with a bald pate and fuzzy ginger-blonde hair. Stuck in his belt was a pistol. Like everyone else in the group he had lost a number of his friends. Some had been shot by the police or the Shabiha while out demonstrating, others had been tortured to death in prison. Mobile phones were passed around and the images of dead friends admired. Abu Kassim, a 19-year old FSA fighter, shared a clip which showed rebels cutting off the heads of two young men in cold blood and placing them on their lifeless bodies the way big game hunters do. The victims were said to have been members of the Shabiha and themselves responsible for a number of deaths. Judge and executioner were one and the same. Another video showed the mutilated bodies of twenty-five men who were also said to have belonged to the Shabiha. "It was us who killed them. I was there. They deserved to be killed," declared Abu Kassim, lighting a cigarette. "But we shouldn't have cut off their heads. That's what the al-Qaida people do, and we don't want to be like them." Another fighter sitting next to Abu Kassim shook his head. "Bullets cost money which we can't afford. Beheading is cheap. So long as nobody is financing us any method is justified."

The group spent hours discussing how to get weapons into the city and which districts were to be liberated first. They argued over whether Assad and his cronies should be killed or tried for war crimes.

"Summary execution," said some; "We must end the cycle of hate," objected others. "We have always lived alongside Christians and Alawis; they too belong to Syria. We should seize only the ones who have committed crimes and take them to court, after which they will receive their just punishment, *inshallah*!" so said a lawyer with the *nom de guerre* of Abu Tarb. While they were arguing and drinking coffee after coffee to dispel their tiredness a dull booming sound rang out. Bazookas were being fired at the neighbourhood from an army base. Everyone jumped. "Fear is our constant companion," remarked Abu Hamid.

Shortly after midnight shots were heard in the immediate vicinity. The insurgents with their Kalashnikovs took up position along the balustrade of the roof. The owner of the building led his wife and children to safety in a neighbour's house. Lawyer Abu Hamid slipped the safety catch off his pistol and placed himself behind the street door, ready in case soldiers or police tried to storm the building. Not until morning dawned did the men retire exhausted to bed.

At the end of October 2012 I visited Aleppo again. War had by then fastened its teeth into the city like a pit bull terrier. Once the rebels had opened hostilities in the city Aleppo had turned into an opposition stronghold and government troops had been surrounding the areas controlled by the rebels, battering them unceasingly with everything at their disposal: artillery, tanks, jet fighters, helicopters. Among the crooked alleys of the historic Old City a cruel war was being fought street by street, the residents trapped in a haze of stray bullets, rockets and grenades. Now that Aleppo had become a war zone bread, the staple food, was in short supply. The rebels had set up some specially trained units to bake flatbreads and distribute them to the people, but that was not enough for everyone. Every day long queues formed outside the few bakery shops still in operation.

My daily routine was to wander for hours through the streets of Aleppo visiting hospitals and morgues. Often I would be invited in by total strangers to have a cup of tea and listen to their stories. Rebels were holed up in many of the houses. In one safe house I saw a rebel sniper dying from a wound to his head given him by a sniper of the Syrian army.

One afternoon as I was walking through the Shaar district a fighter plane roared over the street and fired two rockets at a block of flats. The world went dark until slowly, gradually, a faint ray of sunlight reappeared and groped its way through the clouds of dust. Pieces of masonry and furniture rained down from the sky, then an uncanny silence descended on the street. Human forms could be seen rising out of the chaos like shadows, staggering and coughing.

The inhabitants of the street had been torn away from normal life in the blink of an eye, stunned by the fury of two rockets fired from a Syrian air force plane. The missiles had hit the top floor of a block of flats and flames were pouring out of its windows. The explosion had ripped off balconies, shattered window panes and cracked the walls.

Once the dust had settled and the scale of the damage was discernible people began to sort themselves out amongst the ruins. They peered out of holes in the walls made by flying masonry and shook the dust out of their hair. They called to each other to find out whether anyone had been killed or injured. Some called for help, some threw damaged items down into the street. A one-legged man staggered over the heaps of rubble and leaned against the wing of a car half buried in masonry. "Yes, some people did get killed," cried a man, pointing to a flat with smoke coming out of it.

Ibrahim had been standing in the hall when the rockets burst into the sitting room where his parents were sitting watching television. The explosion had thrown him back against a wall, but he had not suffered any injuries. Now he was standing there on the fifth floor of the burning building while smoke billowed up the well of the stairs and neighbours rushed up and down with buckets of water in a vain attempt to put out the flames. Ceiling beams were glowing and the heat was enough to strike a person in the face and singe his hair and skin. Ibrahim's parents were trapped in the living room and the reek of burned flesh hung in the air. A young man got sick in the stairway. "Was my father a terrorist? Was my mother a terrorist?" shrieked Ibrahim, bursting into tears. "Bashar al-Assad has killed my parents! Why? But why?"

An hour or so later the flames were sufficiently under control for some men to be able to climb from the ruined balcony into the living room. They dragged a charred body from under a table and wrapped it in a blanket, crying *"Allahu akbar!"* as they did so. Twirls of smoke rose from the smouldering corpse and escaped from the blanket. Ibrahim was asked to identify the body but it was so disfigured he couldn't tell whether it was his mother or his father. "Dad? Mum?" he whispered, overcome by shock.

In this war there wasn't even time to honour the dead. Hardly two hours after the air raid the incinerated bodies of Ibrahim's parents were lying in the back of a white delivery van as it tore through the streets of Aleppo with its horn blaring. At the martyrs' cemetery on the edge of town gravediggers were working non-stop in shifts to make room for new burials. Everyone had to act quickly as funerals were often targeted by the army. In the distance helicopters and fighter planes were circling, and columns of black smoke rose in the sky while Ibrahim's parents were placed in an unnamed grave lined with bricks. A relative recited a brief prayer. "I've lost hope of anyone coming to our assistance," said Ibrahim after taking leave of his parents.

"America, Europe, Turkey, the Arab League, they're all watching but none of them do anything."

The victims of war were taken to Dar-al-Shifa, a bomb-scarred hospital a few hundred metres from the front. There Dr Othman bustled to and fro between life and death. He was one of six doctors who had refused to flee from the hospital despite the presence of Syrian army tanks just two hundred metres away. Every minute another wounded person would arrive, brought in on a stretcher, in the back of a lorry or in the boot of a car. Paramedics were there to escort each new case, whether civilian or combatant, to the waiting room, and drag away the dead leaving a wide trail of blood on the tiles. In a quiet nook on the ground floor a doctor was extracting pieces of shrapnel from a girl's hip and she was crying out in pain. Her father was standing beside her, holding her hand and staring at the ceiling fan so she wouldn't see the tears in his eyes. A nurse was massaging the heart of an old woman who had been dragged from under the ruins of her home. A small boy stood traumatized in a pool of blood, calling to his father who was stretched out unconscious on a reclining sun lounger, there being a shortage of hospital beds and stretchers. Near the entrance some dead bodies were lying under white sheets, their hands and feet tied together.

In the midst of the chaos Dr Othman hurried from body to body, a stethoscope dangling from his neck, his overall smeared with blood. He went to attend a man in uniform who was lying on a stretcher with a puddle of blood gathering underneath. This was a Syrian army soldier; dark blood was oozing from a bullet wound in his thigh. Dr Othman administered an injection of adrenalin and inserted a cannula while another doctor eased the bullet out of the wound. Then he hastened to the next case, a woman who had had the back of her head partially ripped off by shrapnel. She was already dead. Dr Othman closed her eyes, then a couple of orderlies wheeled her body to the entrance for her relatives to collect. "It is astonishing how much horror a human soul can bear," remarked Dr Othman. Three months ago when the first air raids had filled the intensive care unit with trauma patients his hands had shaken so much he couldn't manipulate a scalpel. Since then the limit of his endurance had risen a great deal. Still, in his rare moments of rest he had to struggle to dispel some of the ghastly images which had lodged in his brain and prevented him from sleeping properly at night. The dull report of shells exploding had become the sound track of his life.

The hospital had been targeted in air raids on six different occasions, and shells had landed in the immediate vicinity more than twenty times. The upper storeys had been devastated; nobody dared go upstairs any more. The wards were empty, the maternity unit and all its cots destroyed, all the installations and equipment ruined. For Assad's regime even hospitals were legitimate targets.

Dr Othman was a slightly built man dressed in a green lab coat. The neon ceiling lights etched dark rings under his weary eyes and his skin looked as pale as milk. He had hardly slept for days, snatching only a couple of hours' sleep in the basement clinic, not far from dozens of wailing, groaning and dying patients. "We get about a hundred and fifty patients a day. About eighty percent of them are civilians, the rest are rebels or government soldiers."

The doctor leaned against a wall, exhausted. Talking was an effort for him; his eyes were twitching with fatigue. It took him some time to put his nightmare into words. "Most of the wounded require amputations. We need more staff. And yesterday we had a whole lot of dead children," he added, rubbing his eyes. A fighter plane had attacked a baker's shop in one of the suburbs when hundreds of people had been queueing there for bread. "I'm fed to the teeth with war. So much suffering, so many people killed. We are being fired at, bombed and slaughtered. But we shall hold out to the bitter end, until Bashar al-Assad is driven out." He flinched as machine gun fire clattered outside. Some rebels were trying to shoot down a helicopter which was circling over the hospital. Shortly afterwards shells started falling and the next wave of wounded people came flooding into Dr Othman's makeshift operation theatres.

Chapter 5: The Sheikh

I was standing in a pool of blood in Dar-al-Shifa hospital, watching citizens of Aleppo die, when a tall heavily built man clapped his hand on my shoulder. His face was framed in a thick beard and he had a turban on his head. Did he intend to scare me away? Maybe my presence annoyed him, maybe he wanted his people to be allowed to grieve in peace without being filmed by a foreigner. But he was smiling. He grabbed my hand and shook it warmly. "Thank you for taking an interest in the sufferings of my nation," he said, speaking in excellent English. "Where will you be staying tonight?" In fact, I was planning to sleep in the basement of the hospital. "Not safe, my friend. You're going to stay at my place. I won't take no for an answer!"

And that is how I got to know Sheikh Abu Yazan. For the next few weeks I stayed at his small apartment in Tariq al-Bab, a poor, conservative quarter of Aleppo mainly inhabited by Sunnis, and Abu Yazan became my protector, my confidant and friend. The people of his locality addressed him simply as "Sheikh". He was given that title because he had done higher studies and visited Mecca, and because he refused to be cowed by the circumstances of war. He was a figure of authority. In the days to come I accompanied Abu Yazan as he attempted to restore order amid the chaos.

I saw him distribute parcels of provisions to the poor in his area, as he did every week. He was standing at the centre of a cluster of people. A woman swathed in black kissed his right hand as she clutched her food parcel, embracing the black plastic bag as if she would never leave go of it. *"La ilaha illa llahu,"* she whispered. There is no deity but God; but there are covetous people too. Six other hands simultaneously clawed the woman and grabbed at the bag, for inside it was real treasure: a kilo of rice, cooking oil, beans, sugar, salt, two tins of tuna, some dried flatbread and biscuits, enough to ensure another few days of survival, there in the centre of Aleppo.

The woman stepped back, shook herself free and hurried away. Abu Yazan was left standing there, surrounded by dozens of veiled women. "What can I do?" his resigned gesture seemed to ask. A figure in black *jelabia* and greying beard, he had spent that whole morning poring over figures and stocklists in a bombed school building. There were 223 parcels for 654 needy individuals. Now the women were pushing him back against the wall of the small storeroom, begging, cajoling, demanding. "We're hungry!" they cried. One woman lifted up her little daughter and held her to Abu Yazan's chest. "Here, take my daughter, take her home with you!" Just then a bullet whizzed overhead. Was it just a stray bullet from one of the many firing lines around, or had a sniper aimed intentionally at the crowd? There was panic and everyone threw themselves to the ground.

Abu Yazan seized his opportunity, ran out, turned into a side street and soon reached his house. He mounted the stairs to his flat with drooping shoulders, as if bearing an invisible burden. For weeks there had been no electricity or running water in his flat.

Abu Yazan was one of the revolutionaries fighting the Syrian regime without weapons. Instead of shooting people the 46-year old was organizing the community and preparing for the Syria of the future, whilst Assad's regime wobbled (this was in early 2013) but was still far from crumbling. The state was waging war on its own citizens; it attacked and then pulled back, leaving gaps. People like Abu Yazan tried to fill in those gaps.

"I'm an electronic engineer, not a politician," said Abu Yazan as he opened the door of his flat. "I used to have a little shop where I did computer and television repairs." He seemed to be talking of a bygone era. He splashed brownish water from a bucket onto his face and neck. "Earlier on, before fighting started with weapons, when we had just started to risk demonstrating in the streets, we used to hold secret meetings." The conspirators included neighbourhood representatives, former government officials, Islamic scholars, teachers, doctors, students, academics and Muslim Brothers, and in early 2012 they used to meet and discuss what a moderate Islamic republic might look like, how elections could be organized and what kind of punishment would suit the dictator and his men. "At that time few really believed we could reach our goal."

But in summer 2012 war finally came to Aleppo as well. Suddenly refuse collections stopped and shops closed. "You must do something," Abu Yazan had told himself. And so he became an unofficial leader.

He collected money, food and medicines from wealthy Syrian businessmen, Islamic relief organizations and friends. He set up brigades of volunteers to clear the piles of rubbish which by then were shoulder high, got stocks of firewood and kerosene for the cold weather, arranged burials for unidentified bodies, settled disputes between neighbours. There were others like him in other parts of the city. Here and there they set up schools and courts dispensing rudimentary justice. The next thing they were planning was a police force to prevent looting and restore a sense of order and security in the community. Somehow, in spite of everything, they were managing to establish a workable system with schools, courts and neighbourhood offices, a sort of parallel government.

I wondered how, out of the radio technician Abu Yazan, a civilian hero of the Syrian war had come into being. "Maybe it has something to do with my background," said Abu Yazan, and he started to explain.

For decades the people of Syria had lived in peace. True, there was torture and execution back then, but only behind high walls and it only affected the few who spoke out. It was hard to find a middle way between subjection, death or exile, but Abu Yazan's father had found one.

As an officer of the farmers' union in the eighties Abu Yazan's father had striven for better prices and other concerns of the farming community. He could have carved out a prosperous career for himself but he had chosen not to do so. And he could not be bribed. Most significantly, he had made no effort to join the Baath party headed by Hafiz al-Assad, the father of the current president. His colleagues had laughed at him for staying out in the cold, but that was what he chose: a modest lifestyle, preserving his self-respect. When he died three thousand people came to see him off. A similar degree of respect was now shown towards his eldest son, Abu Yazan.

Abu Yazan had been telling his story for one hour. He yawned, pulled himself together as if he had received a shock, and sprang to his feet. It was 2 p.m. by the time when, in his rattling Toyota car, he drove up to a grim block in a district called Hanano. It was the headquarters of the Islamic Front for the Liberation of Syria, a kind of civic council composed of moderate Muslims, Salafists, Islamists and secularists who were determined to establish order in Aleppo. The building had been shelled a number of times, as the crater in the back yard and the pockmarked concrete walls testified. Armed rebels guarding the wrought iron gates were preventing a crowd of desperate people, mainly women with children, from storming the building. "Be patient! Wait for your turn!" cried one guard, blocking an old woman's way with his Kalashnikov. "Please let us in," begged the old woman. "We're afraid of the planes."

Abu Yazan pushed his way through the crowd, scattering them. "We've received a consignment of flour from Turkey." It was important to distribute the rations fairly and prevent squabbling and misuse. A young man was busy filling plastic bags with milk powder in the entrance hall.

Abu Yazan had come to pass judgment in a case. His job, as an Islamic scholar, was to dispense justice in accordance with the Sharia; no normal courts were operating any more. A couple of youths aged 18 and 19 were standing in a side room, shivering all over. Abu Yazan looked them up and down, sat at his desk, flicked through a document and scanned the boys again. "Ho, what have we here? Thieving, I see. Hmm," he muttered, without giving the accused another glance. "And so you were caught in the act."

"Sheikh, please let me explain," begged one of the pair. But Abu Yazan raised a hand telling him to keep quiet. The boy instantly fell silent.

"Now what shall I do with you?" Abu Yazan paused theatrically. "I know! I'll hand you over to the

Jabhat al-Nusra and they can cut your hands off. What do you say?" He winked to his clerk, who giggled to himself.

"Oh Sheikh! No, please don't! We'll never do it again! We are so sorry! Please!" begged the accused.

"You were also found to be carrying weapons," went on Abu Yazan, waving a pocket knife in front of them. "Indubitably a case for al-Nusra. Say goodbye to your hands!"

At that both the youths started to cry. After a while Abu Yazan abandoned his game of bluff and gave the youngsters a twenty-minute lecture: theft was something that undermined the revolution, poisoned the soul and went against the teachings of the Quran. Then he pronounced judgment. "Thirty hours of voluntary service here in this Islamic centre. And I shall have a word with your parents. Report for duty at ten a.m. tomorrow. Now make yourselves scarce!" The two youths crept out of the room, heads bowed in shame. As the door closed Abu Yazan slapped his thigh and roared with laughter. "Of course I would never really have handed them over to the extremists!"

On the way back home Abu Yazan needed to visit a certain family and deliver some relief goods: a plastic bag containing rice, some flatbread, an apple, cooking oil and soap. Stopping in a side street he went down a stairway into the dim basement of a block of flats. A family of nine were living there. Four children were squatting on the damp concrete floor, ghostly, shadowy figures like skinny goblins, arms wrapped around their emaciated bodies against the cold. One boy was suffering from a chesty cough; a little girl was crying. There wasn't even a candle burning; the only illumination was a grey gleam from the well of the stairs. Water was dripping from the ceiling of this dungeon.

The children's mother, who declined to give her names or those of her children for fear of reprisals, was sitting close to them, her face hidden behind a black veil showing only two morosely staring eyes. The head of the family was away fighting somewhere; quite possibly he was already dead. His wife hadn't heard from him in weeks, and the children hadn't been out of their prison for months; not once in that time had they seen sunlight. "I worry about air raids, so I don't let the children out," explained their mother. Not a day went by when their neighbourhood was not shelled, and thus the cold, damp, dark cellar had turned into a refuge from the war raging just overhead. It was five months since the family had retreated there. "We have had hardly anything to eat. We get given some rice, but I sell it because we have no gas to cook it with. See, we have nothing. Not even clothes, not even shoes! My children are sick with cold and hunger. And the youngest is losing her teeth because she's getting no milk," cried the woman in exasperation. Her voice broke and turned into stifled sobbing. Then the dull crash of exploding shells penetrated the cellar. The children crept to the very back of the room, where they merged into the darkness. Quietly and helplessly we took our leave.

Abu Yazan had learned in childhood not to hide from life. His first passion was for kung-fu; later he studied the Quran with similar eagerness. "Martial arts and religion sharpened my mind," he said, explaining how he used to dress like Bruce Lee and attend mosque in the same kit. He followed the Prophet's precept, to constantly educate the soul; to keep learning all through life and to pass on his knowledge. First he had studied biology and electronics, then he had honed his religion at the universities of Damascus, Aleppo and Tripoli. He had studied the Quran and learned it by heart and he had gained a qualification in Islamic studies. By then he felt close to God, and people started calling him Sheikh. He used to teach local children kung-fu and tutored others in biology, English and physics. He did so without remuneration because, he said, "the Quran forbids charging money for passing on knowledge." Every Friday he would give a sermon at the mosque. "It is my duty to do good. That's what the Quran says, and that is the will of Allah." Before the revolution he had kept his family afloat with the income from his little repair shop, located on the ground floor of the block. That was enough to pay the rent for a small flat and let him make a pilgrimage to Mecca. "It was a simple life and a good one." He took on his present role in order to set an example. He had taken on big responsibilities and hoped neither to be crushed by them nor to misuse them.

The reference to getting crushed was no joke. It was early evening of a cold February day in 2013 and Abu Yazan was sitting in his living room, exhausted. The day had been long. He chucked the last log into the stove. Since the electricity supply had gone off people had been cutting down Aleppo's trees and using them for firewood. Abu Yazan's son Mustafa greeted his father, kissed his hand and relieved him of his jacket, then told him the latest bad news. A rocket had hit a residential area in the nearby district of Hanano, a shell had killed nine children in a back street, and in Bustan al-Qasr local people had recovered a hundred and ten corpses from the river Queiq. "All of them had been shot in the head, father, and their hands were tied behind their backs," Mustafa reported. In bizarre contrast to his words the sound of children laughing came from the street below. Abu Yazan's youngest son Qusai was playing a game like marbles with some of his mates; but instead of marbles they were using some empty bullet cases which had rattled down onto the street when an army helicopter had fired at the area. Then a fighter jet roared at low altitude over Tariq al-Bab and Qusai came running up into the flat, crying, and flung himself at his father's legs.

Abu Yazan was a tall, heavy man with kindly eyes which made him look vulnerable. He was a pious

Muslim, moderate, but conservative and traditional in his interpretation of the faith. He was constantly asking himself how to apply the teachings and values of 7th century Islam to modern society, how to reconcile belief and rational thought. He wouldn't be able to put such ideas into practice until the war was over, of course. "But so far Allah has not answered my questions," he admitted. Then his head nodded, his eyes closed and he fell asleep, only to wake with a start when four-year-old Qusai suddenly leaped onto his stomach and shouted "Assad is a donkey! God is great!" Abu Yazan smiled wearily.

In the past the questions which had occupied him had been less existential in nature. Now bombs were falling, bullets were whistling overhead. The whole family was traumatized as a result of the incessant bombardment; his sons woke screaming at night, his daughter went for days without sleeping at all, his wife no longer dared to go out into the street. Was reconciliation possible in such circumstances? "There is no alternative, if we are to save Syria," replied Abu Yazan.

The following morning a second cup of strong black tea banished his weariness for a while. For a long time, he had been sleeping badly – there were so many plans in his head and so many demons lurking in the darkness. He did not really know how reconciliation could be achieved, or what might happen once Assad was gone. Democratic elections? A moderate Islamic state along Turkish lines? Sharia law? Who could say? "At the moment people are busy trying to survive. But whatever happens we mustn't let Assad's dictatorship be replaced by a religious dictatorship as the Islamists want." Bangs and cracking sounds filled the air outside. Abu Yazan smiled contentedly.

"God has a plan for me and I must carry it out," he said. But the responsibility weighed heavily on his shoulders. Especially when, as today, a crowd of war widows gathered outside his gate and he had to send them away empty handed because his supplies had run out. Was he afraid? He paused for thought, then nodded slightly. And then he leaped into his Toyota, ready to visit the war front where three of his four brothers were fighting. His driver was used to dodging death and always knew where snipers were positioned and where fighting was going on. In the back sat Abu Yazan's bodyguard Yusuf, the son of a relative, a slim 22-year old who was clutching his Kalashnikov so tightly his knuckles had gone white. First we called at a secret hospital on the way to the front. I wanted to donate some blood, as Aleppo was running out of reserves.

Dar-al-Shifa hospital, where I had met Dr Othman at the end of July, had been destroyed in November. To replace it a makeshift clinic had been set up in a former shopping centre a few metres away. There we met Dr Abdul standing next to a stretcher with a dead boy lying on it. "Why will nobody help us?" he asked despairingly. He cursed the regime, cursed Europe and America. "By just standing by and watching the world is helping the regime to wipe us out!" He also cursed the local Islamists and foreign fighters pouring into Syria from all corners of the world who were gaining in strength as they occupied the gaps left by other forces and filled them with their weapons and fighters. "Those people are crazy, they are betraying the revolution and betraying Islam. We do not share their view of Islam, but we can't afford to be fussy. We have to accept help from anyone who will give it, since there is no other choice," he said, adding that the Syrian people had no wish to swap Assad's dictatorship for an Islamic one. Meantime a shell had exploded in the Hanano district, and soon afterwards a fresh batch of people with severed limbs and gaping wounds were brought into the mall.

A nurse showed me into a side room and pulled the curtain. While the doctor stuck a cannula into my vein Yusuf enquired anxiously whether the blood of a non-believer would be able to save the life of a Muslim. Abu Yazan gave him a friendly rap on the forehead and told him he need not worry, even a non-believer's blood would be good for Muslims. Immediately the bodyguard embraced me and swore he would protect me with his life from then on.

Abu Yazan's brothers and cousins were fighting in the Karm al-Jabal district, close to the historic Old City. It was a risky business to call on them, and Abu

Yazan had to cross three streets held by enemy forces with snipers among them. "We'll meet up on the other side, *inshallah*," he said as we dashed across with heads down. He used to visit his brothers as often as possible. They had chosen a different form of resistance to him. Two of them served as couriers, moving among the different units holed up in derelict buildings and delivering ammunition to them. The third was the commanding officer of a small platoon which attacked army checkpoints and positions, carried out ambushes and shot at tanks.

"*Salam alaikum*," the brothers greeted each other. "Peace be upon you." They were sitting round a stove in a corner building out of reach of snipers. Bullets whizzed by and shells exploded outside, while in their room the brothers drank sweetened tea, said their prayers together and discussed the casualties in recent days. The fighters were gradually running out of ammunition, but they felt that victory was almost within their grasp. Of course they had been saying the same for months. Recently the government forces had started using scud missiles in an attempt to sap the will of the rebels. Stood on end those missiles were as tall as a house; one was enough to destroy an entire neighbourhood. Hundreds of people had been killed by them in the past week or so. That meant yet more fathers bewailing their sons and women bewailing their husbands. 70,000 dead in two years: how could the country withstand such losses? The answer was silence and an uncertain shrug of the shoulders. Before leaving Abu Yazan wrote "*Allahu akbar*" on the wall with a marker pen: "God is great," he said. "That will protect my brothers." "*Inshallah*," murmured the brothers. But they didn't sound very confident.

After six months of street fighting Karm el-Jabal was a scene of desolation monitored by snipers from both sides of the conflict. All around were collapsed buildings, mounds of rubbish, burned out shops, depopulated areas of rubble. In the bomb-blasted streets lay the rusting wrecks of tanks and the bodies of people nobody dared remove. Shells kept detonating.

Many Syrian army soldiers were deserting and crossing over to join the FSA. A young man in uniform was darting across the road when he was hit in the lower leg by a bullet. He collapsed onto the ground and was dragged out of firing range by another rebel. "He might just as well have hit me in the head," cried the man in his shock. "Then everything would have been over."

"I see our young men fighting all right," murmured Abu Yazan, sitting in the back seat of his old Toyota, "but I don't see them helping the poor. A bullet can end a life swiftly, but the circumstances we are in now derange our minds, kill us slowly from within and poison our souls with fear and hatred."

By that time increasing numbers of foreign combatants were joining the Syrian rebels. At one rebel stronghold I was interrogated by some jihadists

from Azerbaijan who wanted to know what I was up
to in Aleppo. As an unbeliever I had no business
there. They had long black beards and looked
menacing. They kept pointing first at their rifles then
at me. It was the first time I had felt myself to be an
unwanted visitor in Syria. They didn't let me go until
Abu Yazan had vouched for me. On another
occasion a car stopped level with me and its young,
European-looking driver called me over. He
addressed me in English and asked where I was from.
When I told him he laughed in delight and, switching
to German, said he had lived for some time in the
city of Kassel, though he actually came from Kosovo.
He had come to Syria to die the death of a martyr. So
saying he bid me goodbye and drove on. Another
time I was about to take pictures of a group of rebels
when my companion warned me not to. He said they
were fighters from Chechnya and it was wiser not to
film them.

The war had taken on a new hue, and it had
altered Abu Yazan too. He had learned to suppress
his fear, to hold himself at a distance from the
horrors and be pragmatic. He could now distinguish
the different noises of war. He could judge how far
away a missile had landed just by the sound, and tell
whether it was a bazooka or a rocket. Sirens were
part of his daily life and outbursts of fighting marked
the times of day for him. He had taken to wearing a
black *jelabia*, like the Prophet had done 1400 years ago,
and he had let his beard grow as prescribed in the

Quran. Religion offered protection from the madness, traditional clothing was an expression of resistance to the secular dictatorship of Assad. And somehow, for the first time in his life, he felt free, as he told me on the way back from the front. "I can no longer rebel in silence." Many others were thinking the same.

His old suits were in vacuum packs hanging in a wardrobe. His previous life was receding into the dim recesses of memory; he couldn't look back. The war had given him new responsibilities. I asked him why he had taken on so much. "Because I want to set an example for others to follow. This is the only way our society can keep going." And his next task was waiting for him.

In a windowless room in the Shaar district of Aleppo that afternoon Hussein, a young man barely twenty years old, was lying half asleep on a grimy mattress, groaning all the time. His body was emaciated; his bandaged legs had swollen as thick as tree trunks from raging infection. Pus was oozing from the dirty bandages. His back, shoulders and arms were covered in sores as a result of lying motionless on the mattress for months on end.

He had never been a rebel or a combatant, nothing but an ordinary youth. Months earlier, in September 2012, he had gone out to buy vegetables for his mother when a shell had exploded near him and pieces of shrapnel had lodged in both his legs including the thighs, the knees and the feet. At the only remaining hospital in Aleppo the doctors had told his mother that there was nothing they could do for him as their orthopaedic specialists had fled; he would have to be taken to Turkey or some other part of Syria where doctors were still available. But she had no money to pay for the transport, so Hussein had been rotting at home in this dark cell ever since.

A few days before a neighbour had told Abu Yazan about the young man's plight. Since then Abu Yazan had been constantly on his mobile phone, cursing whenever reception went dead for hours at a time. By now he had lined up a surgeon he knew in Idlib and organized an ambulance.

Its siren wailing, the ambulance tore through Aleppo's maze of back streets and out of the city. The journey to Idlib, an area under siege, along roads where sniper bullets and shellfire were a constant threat, was a long and dangerous one. The vehicle raced across the plains of Syria, clocking 120 kilometres per hour to elude hostile fire and making detours to avoid government checkpoints. Twice it narrowly missed being hit. Each time it bumped over a pothole Hussein, in the back of the vehicle, was dislodged from his stretcher and howled in pain. His head was in his mother's lap and she, with tears running down her face, was running her fingers gently through his hair and giving him sips of lukewarm cola to drink.

As dusk was falling the ambulance reached the secret clinic without a name; it was surrounded by olive groves and situated well away from Assad's forces. A surgeon examined Hussein's wounds and shook his head. In such a case there was nothing to do but amputate. Hussein's mother broke down in sobs. The doctor promised to get her son to a hospital in Turkey within a few days. It was late at night when Abu Yazan set off on the return journey to Aleppo. In place of the patient some armed fighters now sat in the back, to defend the vehicle in case it ran into a government road block. "God be with us," breathed Abu Yazan. Death most commonly came by night.

During the night the Syrian air force launched one raid after another. Rebels fired mortars at government positions and tried to bring the planes down using heavy machine guns. The crackling dialogue of weapons continued hour after hour. Morning found Abu Yazan safe home, but he hadn't slept a wink all night. He surveyed his breakfast with weary eyes, then devoured his flatbread and hummus. He smiled kindly at his sons. Suddenly there was a hiss followed by a boom; dust and bits of masonry flew in through the open window. The next house, scarcely five metres away, had been hit by a shell and its top floor destroyed. "*La ilaha illa llahu!*" exclaimed Abu Yazan: there is no deity except God. Soon after that he left the flat; there was no longer a smile on his face.

It was time for me to leave Aleppo. Abu Yazan embraced me in farewell. "May God protect you, brother!" In truth he needed God's protection more than I did. Still, before I got into the rickety Opel which was to take me to the Turkish border I needed to disguise myself. The most dangerous part of my wanderings lay ahead: the way out of Syria into Turkey. All the roads leading out of Aleppo were studded with checkpoints set up by Islamist jihadis. Several journalists had been abducted nearby in recent weeks. I already had a beard and I put on a robe plus a *kufiya*, the traditional Arab male headdress; this disguise was intended to make me less easily recognizable as a foreigner and potential candidate for abduction. Five armed bodyguards provided by Abu Yazan got in the car with me. It was not long before we ran into the first road block. Islamists shrouded in black stood in our way. Without speaking they trained their rifles on our vehicle. My companions slipped the safety catches off their Kalashnikovs; one even drew the pin from a hand grenade. "Don't utter a word! These guys are crazy!" one of the rebels whispered to me as a man in a balaclava searched the boot of the car. A few words which I did not understand were exchanged between the shrouded men and my bodyguards. My nuts were in my throat, but I was in luck; they waved us through. One hour and two roadblocks later I walked over the frontier into Turkey.

Chapter 6: Qalamoun – Damascus, April 2013

Northern Syria was becoming ever more of a no-go area for reporters. By mid 2013 Islamists had abducted dozens of journalists: Spaniards, Frenchmen, Englishmen, Americans, Japanese, even one Russian. They were all heading for Aleppo, hoping to gather material there or in the area round Raqqa. Trafficking agents and spies from Islamist groups would latch onto foreign media people even as they crossed the frontier and ensnare their intended victims within hours. So there were very few people daft enough to venture into the war zone of north Syria.

It was quite simply too dangerous to try getting into Aleppo; the risks were sky high. Abu Yazan had warned me not to attempt it. "Don't come here, brother. al-Qaida and ISIS are in control of all the access roads to Aleppo. I cannot offer you protection." However, there were still other ways of getting inside Syria.

I planned to travel from the Lebanon into southern Syria, into the suburbs of Damascus. Rebels were fighting government troops there too. But it wasn't going to be simple; a long odyssey lay before me, taking me from Beirut to the old Roman city of Baalbek, then on to the Lebanese-Syrian frontier by unfrequented roads. There I would be met by contacts who would spirit me into Syria, illegally and without any visa. That, at least, was the theory of it.

What I was not aware of was that the Syrian army was just then in the process of encircling Damascus and subjecting rebel positions to sustained and merciless artillery attacks and air raids. All access roads were being blocked by checkpoints which constantly changed location. Not a soul was being allowed into or out of Damascus. For some days all of the rebels' supply routes and avenues of retreat had been cut off.

"Come to Baalbek," a contact from a Syrian underground network in Lebanon texted me. In the shadow of some Roman pillars I met the men who were to smuggle me into Damascus. We set off in an old Mercedes, made detours around some Lebanese military checkpoints, crossed the Bekaa valley and finally arrived at the small town of Arsal. That was where almost exactly a year earlier I had met my first Syrian refugees coming to the Lebanon from Homs, Damascus and Qusair. I still clearly remembered the distressed and weeping children being lifted by their distraught parents from the back of a lorry. Now there were thousands of Syrian refugees living in Arsal, taking shelter in stables, crude huts and tents or squeezed in with relatives. The Lebanese people were continuing to help them as best they could. One local man told me he thought it was his duty to make room in his house for homeless people from the neighbouring country, much as the Syrians had done when Lebanon had been plunged in civil war and tens of thousands of people had fled to Syria.

In Arsal we switched vehicles and I boarded a minibus. The man behind the steering wheel was high on adrenalin and had a hand grenade nestling in his lap. We set off. Exhausted yet tense I flopped back against the rear seat. As night fell we were bumping along a cart track over the border. A couple of hours later we reached the town of Yabroud where we stopped at a restaurant for kebabs, washed down with a delicious yogurt drink called *ayran*. "You'd better hurry, the Syrian air force bomb this town every night," the restaurant owner told us. After our meal we drove on, accompanied by an armed escort, until the minibus stopped outside a farmhouse in the middle of nowhere in the Syrian province of Qalamoun. The driver indicated that we had reached the end of our journey.

I found myself in an empty field some thirty kilometres from Damascus. All around there was nothing but fields, orchards and hills. It was like a scene from a picture postcard. I shared a room in a tiny farmhouse on the edge of the city with my escort of five Islamists. Three of them were called Muhammad, which suited me as I'm bad at remembering names. Also present were 22-year old Amir, my driver and interpreter, who had difficulty distinguishing the civil war from a video game, and Abu Ahmad, a preacher who knew the Quran by heart and later kept trying to convert me to Islam.

They were battle-scarred veterans of the fighting in Homs, Qusair and Hama.

My contact in Beirut had warned me about this group of Islamist rebels who were going to receive me and escort me into Damascus, "God willing", but he had urged me not worry. "They're nice people, that lot!" he had assured me, as I formed a mental image of extremists brandishing Kalashnikovs.

My journey to Damascus turned into a journey into the minds of these Islamist rebels. None of them was over 25 years of age, all of them had wild black beards and close shaven hair. In fact, they were pleasant young men, and good fun too. We larked about and got on well with each other. They were far from being venomous, narrow-minded extremists filled with hatred for anything that didn't fit in with their view of the world, they were quite different from what I had imagined. Obviously they objected to alcohol and drugs, nightclubs and free love. So what did they think about sex? It could only take place between husband and wife, Abu Ahmad assured me. As all of them were unmarried that meant they were all living in a state of virginity, unfulfilled – which might explain why they used to stroke and fondle their Kalashnikovs as if they were girlfriends.

People often talk of "the rebels" when discussing the armed opposition in Syria. But there is no single monolithic group of insurgents, instead there are numerous heterogeneous factions, each with its own aims and many in total disagreement with each other. The general category of rebels includes secularists, students, lawyers, doctors, deserters from the Syrian army, peasant lads. Latterly radical Islamists from the shadowy realm of al-Qaida have increasingly been taking a leading role in the civil war, groups like Jabhat al-Nusra and Ahrar al-Sham. All the different factions have one aim in common: to overthrow the dictator Bashar al-Assad. But as to how that end is to be achieved, and what is to happen when Assad is gone, those are matters on which they do not agree. Should there be free elections paving the way to a modern Muslim democracy like that of Turkey, or an Islamic caliphate having the Quran as its constitution and the Sharia as its legal system, or what?

"Are you a Muslim?" one of the Muhammads asked me with a piercing look when we first met. This should have been the cue for a little fib, which in that part of the world could be justified as a necessary form of self-defence. For I am an atheist, and in the eyes of a believer only one thing is worse than worshipping the wrong deity, and that is not recognizing any deity at all. I shook my head. "A Christian?" Another no. He became thoughtful and pulled his beard; his eyes narrowed to slits and he came so close to me I could feel his breath on my face. "Jewish?" My Adam's apple leaped and I croaked, "No. No religion, no god." At that all the men opened their eyes wide in astonishment, then launched into a vociferous argument. It sounded as if my hosts were discussing the best means of dispatching this infidel son of a bitch to the hereafter. I stepped outside to have a smoke and calm my nerves. After a while Amir joined me, silently puffing smoke rings into the night air. My hands were still jittering. Inside the room the argument was going on louder than ever. Amir caught my enquiring look and explained: "They're just arguing about whether to cook chicken or lamb in your honour."

I had got over the first hurdle. Over the next few days I learned what normal life meant for these hosts of mine. Visitors kept coming and going in the room we all shared. A knot of fighters dropped by for a joint prayer session. Later a man delivered a load of weapons and cases of ammunition smuggled in from Lebanon. At one point a donkey cart came trotting along and stopped in the yard. A man jumped down from the driving seat, heaved a massive satellite dish off the cart and, with much fuss and palaver, mounted it on the roof of the building.

The internet, at last. That was the plus side. On the other hand, a parabola glinting in the sun would make an obvious target for Syrian helicopters and fighter planes to shoot at. However, that thought did not seem to bother Amir, the Muhammads or the Preacher. Facebook and Skype offered them a welcome change from prayer and weapon-fondling.

A few days later the next delivery took place – a lorry load of medical supplies. Horsh Arab was constantly being attacked by the army, yet it lacked any kind of hospital where injured people could be treated. Every now and then Mo would drop by. He was an American of Syrian descent who had left the Bronx to come over and join in the revolution. He planned to improve the rebels' fitness by means of a cleverly designed training programme and thereby bring the regime to its knees, though precisely how the fitness training would be organized he would not say; basically, he admitted, he was just a pizzeria baker. Abdul, a policeman, called in on us at supper time every day without fail. He served in the official police force but passed information to the rebels. On the whole I enjoyed having visitors; but every one of them seemed to have an urgent need to impress on this German visitor their strange fascination with the figure of Adolf Hitler. Adolf Hitler, strong man! Adolf Hitler, very good man! Germany? Ah, Adolf Hitler! You not like Adolf Hitler?

At first I displayed weary patience, I argued, I tried to win people over. No, no, Hitler bad man. Very bad. Unfortunately, I can't speak Arabic, so our conversations would limp along awkwardly. I tried comparing Hitler with Bashar al-Assad, and that had some effect, though not a lasting one. "Hitler no good?" they would then query, their faces full of disappointment. Finally, a bearded man I'd never seen before came to visit us and made me lose my temper. "*Salam alaikum!* So, what do you think of Adolf H…" I didn't let him finish his sentence, and went on to break every possible rule of Syrian etiquette. As I was soon to find out, my fulminating tirade was aimed at the very last person I should have picked on. For he was my host, the boss of the Islamist group, leader of all the rebels in the area; the unseen puller of strings, the super-Islamist who had enabled me to slip into Syria and provided me with vehicle transport, bodyguards, food, shelter and an interpreter, all free of charge. He was the one person around whom I should not on any account have offended. A certain coldness and displeasure on his part was the very least I could expect; but the good man simply smiled at me and apologized for having evidently hurt my feelings. To make amends he offered me his pistol as a gift, and here again I ran into a dilemma, and had to shrug off his generous gesture. But at least the subject of Adolf Hitler was banished from then on.

One night Amir and I were standing outside smoking under a starry sky when a great ball of fire shot over our heads, hissing as it went. "Scud," remarked Amir calmly. The launch pad for those missiles was situated just a couple of kilometres away from our hiding place. Every day several of them would be fired at the liberated areas in the north, Aleppo, Azaz, Marea, Deir Ezzor, Idlib, and each time hundreds of people were slaughtered by them.

In the evenings, when the electricity supply failed taking Facebook and Skype with it, we would sit round the glimmering stove wrapped in blankets, sipping sugary tea and having long discussions about the war and about Syria's future. The question I had heard again and again in my travels around Syria was asked here too: Why did nobody offer help? Why did the world stand by and watch the killing? Even Abu Ahmad, the Preacher, closed his Quran and joined in the conversation. "Maybe," I said, "it has something to do with the poor image the rebels have been projecting since all these fanatics came rushing to join them, people who want to create a black and white world where everything is a matter of extremes: *halal* or *haram*, permitted or forbidden, friend or foe, paradise or hell."

I was referring to the radical Islamists and Salafis who had made their way into Syria from Saudi Arabia, Egypt and Qatar, and from Germany, England and Australia, with the aim of conducting a holy war there. Many of them had joined the al-Nusra front, an offshoot of the Iraqi al-Qaida. "Nusra" actually means help or salvation. More recently fighters loyal to the Islamic State had been spreading terror; they despised anyone whose interpretation of Islam differed from theirs.

The vacuum left by the Western powers' unwillingness to get involved was being filled by radicals who had food and money with them as well as weapons and could thus upstage the impoverished and poorly equipped volunteers of the FSA. In cities like Aleppo, Idlib and Raqqa it was no longer the secular tricolour of the old rebels but the black flag of the Islamic State which could be seen flying. The IS was providing for practically all the needs of the population in the liberated areas to the north; as well as food, medicines, blankets and kerosene they were spreading their own world view. In this war the boundaries of good and bad were getting blurred. Assad was being supported by Iran and the Lebanese Hezbollah, some Iraqi militias and Afghans stranded in Iran who had little alternative than to join in the conflict. The extremists were getting their support from Qatar, the Emirates and Islamic NGOs in Saudi Arabia. Whereas the people who were true to democratic principles, the ones who had started the fight for justice and citizens' rights two years before, were getting no help at all and were being squeezed between the other two parties.

"Yes, we are Islamists, in that we follow Islam. But we reject the so-called Islam of the extremists; those people are out of their minds," said Abu Ahmad. After a pause he added, "Yet they are the only people who assist us." The others nodded in agreement. "I hope for a Syria where everyone can live peacefully together, Sunnis, Shiites, Alawis, Kurds, Druses, Christians. We do not wish to exchange Assad for another dictator. That's not what we launched the revolution for," said Amir. "*Allahu akbar*!" murmured Muhammads one, two and three.

God is great. Football is sometimes still greater. One afternoon, some days after I had lost all sense of time,

I saw Amir looking agitated. He was wearing a Barcelona shirt. I noticed that even one of the Muhammads had swapped his *jelabia* for a Madrid strip. It was a Tuesday, day of the return match in the quarter finals of the champions league. "Do you like football?" Muhammad enquired. I nodded eagerly. "Brilliant!" cried Amir, clapping his hands. "Real Madrid or Barcelona?" "Munich, and on rare occasions Dortmund," I replied. Amir looked disappointed. "Ah well! Then today we'll watch Dortmund, and tomorrow we'll watch Munich. You are our guest, after all."

There was frenzied activity all afternoon. Amir had to somehow persuade the owner of a television set to tune it to Dortmund instead of Madrid and hack into a paying satellite channel. We would need a generator too. One was located in a neighbouring village, but there was a slight problem there, as Amir pointed out. To get there we would have to make a detour around an army checkpoint. *"Ma fi mushkila!"* said Muhammad number one, "No problem!" Okay, then. With an *"Allahu akbar"* five men in football shirts, armed with Kalashnikovs and the Quran, squeezed into the car. When I joined them wearing my bulletproof jacket they roared with laughter and pointed to the sky. Allah will protect you, they meant. Then we sped off into the night with no headlamps.

Twenty minutes later we were standing in the living room of a rebel leader they knew. The room was packed with chain-smoking Malaga fans. The flag of the revolution, green, white and black with three stars, was hanging on the wall. Instead of beer there was tea, instead of pizza pistachio nuts, and instead of football songs religious chanting. Lying there on mattresses were two wounded fighters, one of whom opened his shirt and proudly displayed the wound a sniper's bullet had given him. Prayers were said at half time and each goal was hailed with an *Allahu akbar*.

At the very last moment Dortmund won three to two and I performed a dance round our host's living room with Amir and one of the Muhammads.

When I woke the next morning Amir asked me the question he put to me once every twenty-four hours: how about dying together today? "I can take you to Damascus, but we wouldn't survive the trip," he said with a cheerful grin. "Then we could go to God together as martyrs, you and I!" He made this suggestion as if he could think of nothing more delightful than biting the dust as soon as possible. "No, come off it, Amir," I said. It had been a late night with all that football. I shook my head and tried to banish the sleepiness and chill from my limbs. "Not today!"

I did want to get to Damascus, but in one piece. Amir was a person who couldn't sit still, he always wanted to be doing something. Attacking a Syrian army checkpoint for example, or simply scouting out the neighbourhood. And so it was that day. We got on well together. "I want to show you something," he said, hopping from one leg to the other. "Right, go ahead!" A little excursion? Why not. Anything was better than frittering yet another day away on my grubby mattress. It was a cold morning in April, some of the mountain peaks were still glimmering white with snow, but the sun was shining and there was tender blossom on the fruit trees. It was a beautiful day. For a moment I forgot I was in a place where civil war had been raging for two years and had claimed over a hundred thousand lives.

Amir quickly stuck a few more bullets into the magazine of his Kalashnikov before slinging it over his shoulder and jumping into the car. Two of his mates accompanied us. We drove up a mountain track, higher and higher, over scree and gravel, into a desert zone where not a single tree was growing, not a bush, not a blade of grass. An icy wind was blowing over the barren slopes. "Look, there's Damascus airport down there. We will soon have taken control of that," said Amir, pointing southwards into the hazy distance. I strained my eyes but could not make anything out.

Just then a helicopter appeared in the sky.

I stood on the hilltop as rigid as a gravestone, my head drawn into my neck. Air raids and casual gunfire were a constant threat in Syria and could happen anywhere, any time. The front might be ahead of you one day, behind you another, sometimes to the left, sometimes to the right.

Probably the pilot was simply reconnoitring the area. He circled over us, came down lower, scrutinized us. We were walking targets with nowhere possible to hide on that bald mountain top. But neither Amir nor Muhammad was at all worried. They danced around in circles praising God and aimed their weapons at the copter, which slowly edged away, then they shouted after it, Assad is a donkey.

"Stop that racket!" I shouted irritably, pulling on my bulletproof jacket.

"Are you afraid, press reporter?" asked Amir.

"Yes I am, dammit!" I cried, pointing at the helicopter.

"No point in being scared. Either Allah will protect us or else we'll all go to paradise together as martyrs."

That's wonderful, Amir, an excellent argument. I reminded him I wasn't a Muslim, and said I wanted to be around to watch the football again in the evening; my paradise was a worldly one.

Amir realized I was getting cross and capitulated. We drove back to Horsh Arab, where he decided to visit a family he knew. While we were sitting in the front garden drinking coffee a shell came sailing by, slicing through the air with a whistling sound, and exploded nearby. Another came, and yet another. In my terror I spilled the coffee all over my trousers. Women came rushing out of their houses, eyes wide in fear, dragging their children behind them and seeking shelter in cellars and in a nearby mosque. The noble idea of heading straight for heaven as martyrs evaporated at the sound of approaching shells, and even Amir was shown to possess the instinct of self-preservation. "Allah!" he cried, and we all dashed in panic to take shelter in the barber's shop over the road. There I squeezed into the tiny toilet room with three other men, while outside the world seemed to be coming to an end. The shell bursts were moving nearer and arriving at ever shorter intervals. One shell hit a nearby house sending clouds of dust and bits of masonry through the open doorway. We coughed and clung onto one another, jumping every time there was an explosion. Wheeee ... boom! Wheeeee ... boom! Five, six, seven shells, landing hardly twenty metres away from us. The walls of the barber's shop trembled, and so did my knees. Strange thoughts raced through my mind: Should I run away or stay put? Was the place just hit by a shell most likely not to be hit again, or might a second shell land exactly where the previous one did? These were crazy moments filled with the fear of not surviving to see the morrow.

Suddenly everything went quiet. Amir's hand appeared from nowhere, grabbed me by the arm and pulled me out of the restroom and towards the car. We quickly made our getaway and raced out of town; behind us we could hear the Syrian army's bombardment of Horsh Arab start up again. We stopped and hid in a barn in a field. The attack lasted an hour. Miraculously nobody was killed or injured.

"*Al-hamdu lillah*!" said Amir, God be praised. He addressed a quick prayer to heaven.

In the evening Bavaria wiped the floor with Barcelona. After the programme had finished Amir switched to the news on Syrian state television. There were gruesome images of mutilated and dead people, most of them young men, some with their hands tied behind their backs. There were ruined houses and rejoicing soldiers. An off-screen commentator announced that the glorious Syrian army had that day killed many terrorists in Horsh Arab. This was pure propaganda; for nobody at all had been killed in the attack on Horsh Arab. Then the generator ran out of fuel.

Two days later I called off my journey. Rumours were circulating that Hezbollah fighters from the Lebanon were entering the theatre of war. There was talk of more road blocks, and it was clear that my escape route might be cut off if I delayed any longer.

There was no prospect of getting into Damascus anyway. So my Islamist companions took me back to the Lebanon. I was still not ready to give up altogether; it annoyed me not to be able to carry out my plans. In the historic Lebanese town of Baalbek I met up with the Syrian activists who had organized my journey to Horsh Arab. Instead of going to Damascus I now thought I would visit the beleaguered town of Zabadani, just over the mountains which separate Lebanon and Syria.

Zabadani was a mountain spa in whose cool upland climate rich Damascenes used to spend the hot summer months before the war, living in private villas. For the past two years the area had been ring-fenced by the Syrian army. When I reached Baalbek it first started to rain and then the rain turned to snow. It would have been impossible to cross the mountains in such weather. Then when the sun reappeared a few days later the smuggler who was to get me over the frontier started playing silly games. As soon as I had agreed a fee with him he would demand more money. His prospective charge doubled by the hour: first it was two hundred dollars, then four hundred, soon after it was one thousand. In the end he was demanding two thousand dollars for the return trip. The higher he raised his fees the less I trusted him – a man to whose hands I was going to have to entrust my life. In the end I abandoned the idea of going to Zabadani too. Frustrated, with the bitter taste of failure in my mouth and several thousand euros poorer, I slunk back home.

Chapter 7: Zabadani, July 2013

In July 2013 I embarked on a new attempt to get into
the outskirts of Damascus. I had been planning the
voyage for three months, discussed the details on
Skype with Syrian underground activists, sought
interpreters, conducted negotiations, made
preparations, adjusted this and that. What I wanted
was to report on how people were managing to
survive in a city that had been under a blockade for
two years and in which death waited at every turn.
How were essential supplies being brought in? What
kind of public services were still running? Who was
upholding law and order? What were people living on,
how were they surviving? These are important
questions, I told myself. But if I'd known what I was
letting myself in for I would never have embarked on
such a journey.

Everything seemed to have been properly planned.
The smuggler's fees had been successfully negotiated,
fortune seemed to be smiling. In the one and only
cafe of a dusty hole two hours away from the
Lebanese capital of Beirut I met my contact man – a
wiry fellow in dark glasses whose efforts to be
unobtrusive were themselves highly obtrusive. He sat
down beside me, lit a cigarette, blew the smoke into
my face, took off his sunglasses and gazed into my
eyes – all without uttering a word. It was like a scene
in a second rate detective film, and I couldn't help

smiling. I put on my own shades and lit my own cigarette, and then both of us burst out laughing.

The briefing lecture was short. "Listen," said Fadi, for that was the smuggler's name, "in half an hour my cousin Aiman will turn up, and he will drive you to the border. There a car will be waiting ready to take you to Zabadani." The roads were safe, he assured me. Just 22 years old, he was from Zabadani himself but had fled from there to the Lebanon. "It'll take just a couple of hours. You'll be in Zabadani by the evening," he said confidently. Quite straightforward, no question.

Two hours? In a car? I stared at Fadi in disbelief. "What about army checkpoints? I thought the roads were all blocked, I thought we'd have to walk to Zabadani," I objected. Still, I was glad to think I wouldn't have to hump my heavy luggage over the mountains on foot.

"Journalist man, do you not trust me?" pouted Fadi.

"Er, hmm ..." I replied.

"No checkpoints, no army, the roads are safe. Guaranteed," said Fadi with a sweet smile.

As a parting gift he offered me a valuable bit of advice. "Don't tell anyone you're a reporter. There are spies all around," he whispered loudly in my ear. He ordered another espresso before leaving me to meditate on my own – and settle the bill.

Three hours later a black Mercedes with a tinted windscreen drew up, tyres squealing, in front of the cafe. Lebanese pop music wafted out of the open windows. A head, very much like that of Fadi, stuck out and a voice hailed me above the din of the music: "Hey, journalist! Jump in!" So much for the idea of keeping my identity secret.

Not long afterwards I found myself sitting in a hideout on the Syrian-Lebanese border, a little smugglers' den deep in the mountains. From here weapons, food supplies, medicines and journalists were hustled in one direction, refugees in the other. The house was surrounded by high walls. Two battered motorcycles were parked in the yard and two cheerful men were waiting in the house – it was they who would escort me to Zabadani. Aiman greeted them, dollar notes changed hands. Business seemed good, the gravy train had arrived. My chaperones declined to reveal their names, but they were brothers – one tall and thin, the other short and plump. Both of them had long beards. They were wearing combat fatigues and ammo belts and toting Kalashnikovs. And neither of them knew any English, which made communication difficult as I don't know Arabic either.

"Where's my interpreter?" I asked Aiman. The tall thin man went into fits of shrill laughter. When he had composed himself he explained that the interpreter had backed out, as his mother had forbidden him to travel to Zabadani. "Too

dangerous," agreed the plump one. He raised his
Kalashnikov and went "Zabadani – boom! boom!"

They said I needn't worry, with them I was in safe
hands. I wasn't entirely reassured.

"So when will we get to Zabadani?" I asked.

"In a couple of hours," replied the plump one.
"Inshallah."

"By car?" I persisted.

"Car?" Both men bent double with laughter.
"What car? There aren't even any roads here, man!"
Aiman stared at the ground in embarrassment, and
then took his leave.

We drank tea, waited, had a smoke, drank more
tea, waited some more, smiled at each other, sat in
silence. Thus the hours passed, "lost in translation".
At last the smugglers grabbed my baggage and
clamped it onto the motorbikes out in the yard. A
sack full of ammunition was loaded on too. Then we
set off. We jolted over a hilly no man's land,
following cart tracks and paths, sometimes skirting
the burned out wrecks of vehicles shelled by the
Syrian army. After a few kilometres the brothers
halted and said, "Welcome to Syria!"

It seemed crossing the border was a happy event
for my rustlers. They started firing madly at
imaginary targets on a hillside with their rifles. An
anxious shepherd ran for cover. The two brothers
thought all this was hugely funny; I didn't. I imagined
army patrols, helicopters and fighter planes being
attracted by the noise. Target practice in such

circumstances didn't strike me as a brilliant idea. But tall-and-thin and short-and-plump had a more relaxed view of things.

When at last their merry games were over we carried on. Then one of the motorbikes spluttered to a halt. It was out of fuel. The brothers pushed both bikes into a hollow under a projecting rock and camouflaged them with branches. I couldn't make out the reason for not letting the second bike bear the load of luggage and ammunition, but from then on we were reduced to walking – over mountain passes at two thousand metres altitude – with thirty kilo loads on our backs.

As darkness fell we reached the first town of any size. It was under Syrian army control. An all-terrain vehicle was waiting for us in an orchard. "Hurry up, hurry up!" cried the driver, a nervous looking lad who can hardly have been over sixteen. We leaped into the back, where my companions changed into T-shirts and jogging pants and threw a tarpaulin over me and my baggage. We were taken to the house of an underground activist where we hid until late at night.

I was handed over to a different group of smugglers plus four rebel fighters to see us safely out of the town. The fighters thought it unwise to move under a full moon on a cloudless night, but the smugglers were keen to get to Zabadani, and their money, as soon as possible.

"It's too risky. Better wait till tomorrow night," said the leader of the rebels. "*Ma fi mushkila*," replied one of the smugglers; oh, there's nothing to worry about. As a precaution a scout was sent ahead, and after a couple of hours he returned to tell us that our route was "fairly safe and fairly dangerous." We decided to ignore his cryptic analysis and set off at eleven p.m.

I soon realized that the rebel leader had been right. It dawned on me, after I had positioned myself belly down in mire on the edge of a pond, that I was in a serious mess. The man on my left released the safety catch on his Kalashnikov, the one on my right stuck his forefinger in the detonator ring of a hand grenade. My clothes went on soaking up cold water. "Psst!" went the rebel leader, finger on lips. "What's up?" I whispered. But explaining things in advance was never a strong point with my guides; as a rule, I never found out what was happening until long after it had happened.

The full moon was scattering silver on the apricot trees and on the pond where we lay. The tiniest movement sent tell-tale ripples over the water, and the moon was picking us out like a searchlight. "Ambush!" whispered the chap with the hand grenade, pointing into the darkness. I couldn't make anything out. Were we in a trap? The very thought of it made me feel weak. Fear rose in my chest and my teeth chattered so loudly I feared they might give us away.

I have no idea how long we lay there in the mud. Maybe it was a few minutes, maybe an hour or more. I had lost all sense of time and was pondering the odds of surviving to see another day.

There was a rustling in the undergrowth. Barely a hundred metres away figures emerged from the night. The rebels cocked their rifles and took aim; they were all ready to fire. I held my breath. I could hear the beat of my heart pulsing in my ears and I felt small, vulnerable and totally helpless. What the devil was I doing there? After advancing a few metres the Syrian soldiers turned away and all I could hear was their footsteps, a twig cracking under an army boot, a subdued curse. Then they were gone. Full of relief I laid my face in the mud.

For safety's sake we lay there without moving for another twenty minutes. Then a scout was sent out to spy the land. Another half an hour and he returned: the coast was clear. There was a sigh of relief, the men giggled and relieved the tension with jokes. "Hey, journalist, did you get scared?" The same old question, as if they themselves had not. Ha! Very funny. My knees were shivering. When my companions had finished making fun of me we continued our journey on foot.

There was no other way to get to Zabadani. Despite Fadi's assurances all access roads were barred and controlled by the Syrian army. I asked the rebel leader how long it would take us to reach our goal. "Two hours, God willing," he whispered. For a brief moment I had a strong urge to punch him in the nose.

Hour after hour we walked on, through orchards, along deserted railway tracks, over fields. We skirted an army checkpoint, coming so close I could hear the laughter of the soldiers. We darted over a main road next to which one of the rebels fell into a drainage channel and bloodied his nose. We trudged up hill and down. At one stage the rebel leader lost his bearings. Then beside a ruined house in the mountains I threw up, sick with exhaustion. The dull boom of exploding tank shells could be heard in the distance. "Zabadani!" said one of the smugglers, pointing south to where the explosions were lighting up the sky like bolts of lightning.

At last, at five in the morning, we reached the beleaguered town. Going down into the valley was like stepping into a cold bath. Rebels with motorbikes were waiting at the edge of town. The darkness melted away and in the cold light of dawn we drove through a devastated landscape where on every side were ruined houses, wrecked tanks and mounds of rubble.

"Quick, come inside, shells are falling!" someone yelled. I threw down my rucksack and dashed panic-stricken to seek shelter in the entrance of a nearby block. Cramming my helmet on my head I awaited the explosion, heart racing. "Just joking, friend!" said the man with a chuckle. "Welcome to Zabadani, Christian man! I am Fadi's uncle. You're going to be staying with me."

The joker's name was Abu Jaber. He took my rucksack and led me to his flat on the ground floor. All the upper storeys had been bombed to bits. Six rebels were asleep on the couch and floor in Abu Jaber's tiny flat. The room smelled of sweat and cheesy feet.

I was so exhausted I just lay down next to one of the sleeping men and dozed off at once. When I woke it was to see Abu Jaber's smiling face inches away from mine. "Breakfast?" he asked.

Abu Jaber was 36 years old. Before the war he had been an electrician. In typical Islamist style his hair was close shaven and he had a bushy black beard. He was a commander in Ahrar al-Sham, the Freemen of Syria, an radical Islamist splinter group of the Free Syrian Army. He never really knew his father, who back in 1982 had disappeared while in custody following the Salafi uprising in the town of Hama. As with so many of those who rose against the regime he had been arrested and then had vanished from sight. Ten thousand people were said to have perished in the massacre which followed that uprising. "My father was a small-time preacher, that's all," said Abu Jaber. "Maybe he's still alive. However, I doubt it, as we never heard from him again."

Like his father Abu Jaber had also been in prison. He was arrested for having the temerity to demonstrate for more freedom and for the right to follow his Sunni faith. "This is how I paid the price," he said, pulling up the legs of his uniform trousers. The calves, shins, ankles and feet were dotted with small imperfectly healed scars. "That's where they burned me with cigarette butts; this is where they punctured me with a hand drill; and that's where they applied electric shocks." The men who tortured him kept saying, "So you want freedom, do you?" As soon as the first armed resistance groups were formed at the end of 2011 he joined and later became a commander of Ahrar al-Sham with its Islamist bent. Since then he had been active in combat. He certainly wasn't going to let himself be jailed again, he said.

He was an Islamist, there was no doubt about that, but not a terrorist. "Why do people in the West imagine we're out to bomb civilians simply because we believe in Allah?" I didn't want to risk offending my host so soon, yet I couldn't hold my tongue. "Maybe because in recent years, hundreds of videos have appeared on the internet showing Islamists executing people and cutting the hearts out of dead soldiers' bodies," I countered. "Or because Christian villages are being attacked and captive soldiers beheaded." Abu Jaber scratched his head. Yes, something was wrong there. "But it's al-Qaida who do those things, and we have nothing to do with them. They are enemies of Islam. Quite possibly there will have to be a showdown with them once Assad has been deposed. But at the moment they're the only ones fighting on our side." They were a necessary evil.

As was the case almost everywhere in Syria the rebel groups in Zabadani were a mixed bag with different goals, often on bad terms with one another. Abu Jaber had long lost interest in the minutiae of international politics; his world stretched no further than the battered streets of his own home town where sniper bullets provided the sound track. "Come along, I'll show you round," he said. But it was not to be. "*Qasf! Qasf!*" crackled his radio, for like most of the remaining citizens of the town he carried a walkie-talkie with him all the time. Shelling! The Syrian army had resumed its bombardment of the town from its positions on the mountainside. Our tour of the streets had to be postponed.

For the first two days the strafing was so heavy we couldn't step outside Abu Jaber's home. Luckily my friendly Islamist knew all about satellite reception, so at least we had the internet and could spend time on Facebook and Skype. Otherwise we used the computer and played games. My companions were frequently busy praying or cleaning their weapons. I spent a lot of time tossing to and fro on a badly stained mattress; failing to concentrate on reading the books I carried over the mountains. Boredom half killed me, fear kept me awake.

Once a shell exploded so close to the house that fragments from it severed the electricity supply. We spent the rest of the day sitting in semi-darkness staring at the ceiling. Abu Jaber saved food scraps to feed a thin traumatized cat which had been hiding in one of his boots; he stroked her fur and tried to calm her, but without success. In the evening he talked on the phone to his two children who were in a refugee camp in the Lebanon. Yes, daddy is all right, daddy misses you, daddy will soon come and visit you. He laughed when his son begged him to catch "donkey Assad" and put an end to the war. "Daddy loves you. *Salam alaikum,*" he ended. He hung up and turned his head away so I wouldn't see his tears.

It never ceases to amaze me what the human psyche is capable of. Over the next few days I actually got used to the shelling. When missiles exploded outside and the electricity went down, when we were cut off from the world wide web, we sat in Abu Jaber's living room, drank sweet tea and had long conversations about the war and about Syria's future. Yet again I heard the question people always asked me on my travels through Syria: Why does nobody help? Why does the world sit by and watch the killing?

Another morning dawned. As usual we were woken by Assad's shells. "Hurry up, Christian," called Abu Jaber. "I want to show you something." He was standing over my mattress and sounded excited. He pulled the sheet off me.

"Can't it wait?" I groaned.

"The shells are falling far away from here, don't worry."

I tried to be comforted by his words, but failed. Whenever I went out of the house I insisted on putting my bulletproof jacket and helmet on, a habit which sent my companions into fits of laughter. "Are you scared, Christian?" they would ask. Then, pointing at the sky, they would explain: "If Allah wants you to die, you will die. And if he wants you to live he will protect you. It's as simple as that." Then in chorus they would shout "*Allahu akbar!*"

God might be great, but my fear was greater. Unlike my guards I reckoned a martyr's death was not worth aiming for. Nor did I share my new friends' world view. As in Horsh Arab, at first I only gave evasive replies to their questions so as not to be dismissed out of hand as a decadent infidel. Did I drink alcohol? Had I had pre-marital sex? Did I eat pork? Did I frequent bars and nightclubs? Only after a few days had passed did I dare to answer "yes" to any of these questions. Then their first reaction was an embarrassed silence, after which one of them would clap me on the shoulder and say, "Then you'll go to hell, my friend!" It can't be much worse there than here, I would joke, hoping to clear the air. Then there would be laughter, slaps on the back and a peck on either cheek. But I really ought to quit smoking, Abu Jaber advised. Smoking was bad for the health. As if airborne shrapnel was any better, I thought.

The day came when the soldiers in the hills were kind enough to take a break, and I could step outside without qualms. We raced through the town on Abu Jaber's moped, hoping we could move faster than a sniper could take aim. Volunteers were clearing rubble from the streets and sweeping up pieces of shrapnel. "We need to keep the streets clear so that we can make a quick getaway if we're attacked," yelled my bearded companion as we hurtled along. We stopped at the headquarters of his unit. Abu Jaber proudly showed me his arsenal of home-made rocket launchers, mortars, shells and boxed ammunition. "We have just about enough weapons and bullets to defend ourselves, but not enough for an assault." In a side room which was serving as an improvised prison sat two Syrian army soldiers. There were no bars and no lock, only the prison guard, a beefy yob who never stopped smoking. There was nowhere for them to escape to anyway. "Take a film of them," cried the rebels, pushing me into the room. "Go on! Go on!" they urged, acting like big game hunters showing off a trophy. I refused politely and muttered something about the Geneva conventions not allowing people to film prisoners of war because they too had human rights. The only reaction to that was a blank look of incomprehension. But, I said, I would welcome a chance to interview the detainees – in private. In private? No sir, no way.

On the way back home Abu Jaber stopped outside a five storeyed building in the town centre. This was

Zabadani's old police station, he explained. A regime flag was flying from the roof and a picture of Hafiz al-Assad, the father of the current president, was hanging on the facade. There were still a dozen or so police inside. Behind a barrier of sandbags and barbed wire at the gate stood a constable, who waved wearily towards my camera. The rebels had turned the tables, and the custodians of regime law and order were themselves now in custody. However, rebels and police were observing a sort of non-aggression pact. "They do us no harm and we do them no harm. We allow them to come out and shop every day so that they won't starve," said Abu Jaber. And in fact their presence made things a bit safer, as the army tended not to shoot at their own supporters.

On the morning of the third day I met Nermin, Omar and Momin. 31-year old Nermin was editor in chief, reporter and cartoonist of *Oxygen*, a 32-page revolutionary magazine; Momin and Omar were reporter photographers. Nermin together with four of her female friends had founded *Oxygen* when the uprising against the regime was just starting. It was a time when suddenly everything seemed possible and they could at last say and write all that was seething inside them without the fear of having their work censored or being thrown into prison. A time when people like them were taking to the streets, first in hundreds, then in thousands and ultimately in hundreds of thousands, to claim their rights and freedoms; they hoped to end the dictatorship of the past forty years and dreamed of new beginnings. Free thinking in a free press, that was something unknown until then in Syria.

Two and a half years on, with 110,000 people killed, the dream of freedom was almost buried under the rubble of war. But Nermin was still there. She looked demure and wore a head scarf as custom in conservative Zabadani demanded. She was unwilling to give me her real name, for she had to protect herself and her family from the Syrian army and secret police who were looking for her and had put a price on her head. For the last few months she had been living with relatives in a nearby town which wasn't being shelled so frequently. She came to Zabadani only for investigative work and to finalize publication.

Each time she had to risk her life. That morning she had come through two army checkpoints praying to God her inner anguish would not be visible to the soldiers. For in her bag she had a folder containing some cartoons lampooning Assad which she had drawn herself and which were to appear in the next edition. "If they'd seen those I'd be dead or in prison by now," she said faintly. She took out the folder and showed me a dozen cartoons laying bare all the agony of her homeland. She felt her work played an important role in the service of truth. Hers was a high wire act without any safety net. "But luckily the army checkpoint guys seldom take much notice of women," she said, and a smile crossed her face. That was one small triumph.

We walked through the town looking for people who might tell us their harrowing tales. We passed a burned out tank, clambered over heaps of rubble. Nermin stopped and pointed at a ruined building. "That was my parents' house," she whispered. Very few people were venturing into the streets; there was little life to be seen. Nermin, Omar, Momin and I seemed to be the only people around. I felt like an extra in one of those films about doomsday. We crept along like shadows clinging to the walls so as not to offer an easy target to snipers, and darted across open roadways.

Momin told me that Zabadani had been the first Syrian town to be "liberated". That was in January 2012. But its citizens were hardly in liberty, for Zabadani had been under siege ever since. There were army tanks and artillery positions in the hills all around the town and they never paused in their onslaught, firing seventy or eighty shells every day. This bombardment had gradually been knocking down the buildings storey by storey: there was hardly a block left with its upper levels still intact. Eighty percent of Zabadani had been destroyed and the few remaining inhabitants had to seek shelter in cellars or ground floor rooms.

We visited the burned out mosque, then the nearby church whose bell tower had been hit by a shell. Momin filmed the scene while Nermin made notes. "Christians and Muslims lived amicably side by side in Zabadani for centuries," said Momin. "Now our places of worship lie in ruins." He was a thin amiable man with bushy hair who spoke little and spent much time counting his prayer beads. Next to the chancel of the church was a box full of Christmas decorations, a reminder of happier days. Omar pulled out some boxes wrapped in gift paper. "Merry Christmas," he joked, wiping a tear from his face. His voice broke and he started weeping. "We always used to celebrate Christmas along with the Christians," he said. "I miss all that. This war, I can't stand it."

We continued our walk. A man's face appeared at a shattered window and yelled down at us to take cover. "*Qannas!*" he cried. "Sniper!" Then he drew back into the ruin. Shortly afterwards came a message from a lookout in the mountains who was monitoring the army's movements. "Shells! Shells!" crackled Omar's radio. We ran inside the entrance lobby of a block to await the first onslaught. After a bit we moved on, running fast, instinctively bending our bodies low as if that could save us from flying pieces of shrapnel. We took refuge in a flat. Nermin leaned against the wall, trembling, panting for air. "When will all this stop?" she asked, as she closed her eyes.

She sat still, shoulders sagging, her silence underlined by a lull in the bombardment. Then it came again, the shrill scream of a shell followed by an explosion, quite near this time. The minaret of the mosque had been hit. Chunks of brick and plaster and slivers of shrapnel rattled against the outside wall and clouds of dust swept in through the window.

I asked the three reporters why they kept risking their lives, why they didn't flee to Lebanon or Turkey. "Because this is my calling," replied Nermin with fiercely blazing eyes. "Because of this," said Momin, pulling up a trouser leg. His foot, calf and thigh were all peppered with scars. "Electrodes and cigarette butts; a souvenir of prison. My reward for demonstrating."

Little remained of the euphoria of the early days when the demonstrations had turned into a revolution but not yet a civil war. Lively hopes of a new beginning had faded into hopeless resignation. The life they had once known no longer existed and nobody knew what to expect of the future. All that was left was anger, and a defiant determination not to yield to the relentless bombardment. There was also a conviction that right was on their side. As if caught in a treadmill the three of them just carried on, week after week, fighting injustice by the pen.

"It isn't only the regime we're criticizing, it's the armed groups too," said Nermin. "They have hijacked our revolution and betrayed the principles for which we demonstrated in the streets." In nearly every edition of *Oxygen* there are articles about rebels looting, killing civilians or fighting one another. Nermin's biggest worry was creeping radicalization within the armed opposition. People like Abu Jaber, my Islamist friend — who had refused to accompany us because there was a woman in the group. "How did we let al-Qaida slip into our ranks? And by what right do some rebels summarily execute people? Such things make us no better than the enemy we are fighting." Because of her views Nermin was often vilified in the streets of Zabadani and on the internet; she was seen as a traitor and a liability. The new ruling clique did not take kindly to criticism.

I toured the town with Nermin, Momin and Omar for two days. We visited the community kitchen where young men who had never cooked an egg before stewed whatever was available in a large cauldron and distributed it to the needy. We met a farmer in his fields at the edge of town which were strewn with ash and cinders and could no longer be cultivated because the army kept blitzing them. "Assad wants to starve us out," he told me, handing me a shrivelled peach. Asking us to wait a moment Omar disappeared into a nearby house. Half an hour later he reappeared holding up one of his fingers with a loop of wire around it. "I just got married," he announced. In Zabadani sanity and madness were pretty well inseparable.

We often got lost in our own thoughts. Tension and fear would take over my mind; my brain would switch to autopilot. The instinct of survival stood in the way of my duty to ask questions and interview people. Suddenly I was no longer an observer but part of the action, one of the victims, experiencing for myself what it was like to live in a beleaguered town. Priorities were forgotten. Often we just sat silently together with beating hearts, holding hands and counting the explosions. At such times we felt very close; the gap between reporter and protagonist disappeared.

Each evening Momin, the man of few words, would drop in at Abu Jaber's to make sure I was all right. Sometimes he would bring a spraycan of mosquito deterrent, sometimes an apple or an ice cool cola. He once managed to get hold of a kebab, which I devoured eagerly. Sometimes he simply kept me company. "I want you to remember me," he said. These samples of the old civility for which Syria had been famous were an attempt to restore a semblance of normality to the nightmare of our days.

One morning Momin came at six a.m. and shook me from sleep. He said he wanted to introduce me to someone. Zabadani was still asleep and so apparently were the guys in the army tanks. This was the safest time of day, Momin assured me. We stopped outside a house in the town centre with shell-blasted ruins all round. Mariam and her husband Khaled (they were unwilling to tell me their family name for security reason) were kneeling on the living room floor with stencils and pens spread out in front of them. They were designing graffiti slogans for the following day. One said "NO wars of religion in Syria," the other "This is a revolution against a regime." This was their way of contributing to the resistance peacefully and without weapons, like Momin. "Words and ideas are more powerful than a rifle in the long run," said Khaled. Their daughter Shahed was sitting watching while their son Yusef messaged his friends on Facebook until the electricity was cut off. Through the living room window we could see the Syrian army tanks on the opposite mountainside.

Ever since a shell had smashed their own flat the family had been living in this house; it belonged to friends of theirs who had fled from Zabadani. Khaled was about to go out and write his graffiti on the walls as he did every morning. His wife and children would stay at home, for the streets were too dangerous. In one hand Khaled had a bucket containing the charcoal with which he drew his slogans. He tested the batteries of his radio, hugged his wife, kissed the children and set off; Momin and I followed him.

Walking openly down the street was too risky to try. We made detours, clambered over walls, crossed gardens, passed through deserted buildings with holes knocked in their walls to enable people to move around under cover in safety.

Khaled led us up flights of stairs to the fifth floor of an abandoned building to show us his old apartment. The door was off its hinges, but he had fastened it with a padlock. The inside of the flat looked like a bomb site. Unfortunately, Momin had been wrong about early morning being safe; just as

Khaled was showing us his living room a shell whizzed past and landed in the garden with a loud bang. "*Al-hamdu lillah!*" gasped Khaled; "*Allahu akbar!*" murmured Momin; damn bastards, I thought. A warning came over the radio: the tanks have resumed their bombardment of the town. When we reached the street we saw a man lying there in a pool of blood with shrapnel wounds in his head. He was dead. Momin recorded the scene on film.

We sheltered in a neighbour's house while three more shells landed. Khaled was wondering which location to choose for his graffiti that day. On the one hand he rather wanted the Syrian troops to be able to see his slogans, but on the other hand he needed to avoid becoming a target himself. He began sketching on a wall. Now and then he paused and looked up at the hillside to see if there were any suspicious signs of activity. He was ready to dash for cover at any moment. But most of the time he relied on the lookouts who were concealed in buildings and on the hillsides and used walkie-talkies to pass on news of every movement the army made. At last the graffiti was complete. In Arabic script two metres high and two metres wide, it was unmissable. It asked the Western powers and the UN why they stood watching while Syria was being annihilated.

"They've been shooting at us and killing us ever since we first took to the streets. Yet the world still thinks we're a bunch of terrorists," lamented Khaled as he admired his work. "We're a nation which is fighting to save its country." A quick photo shoot for his website and for Facebook, then Khaled started wiping the slogan clean with sponge and water. "We always rub them out straight away, otherwise people will accuse us of being the reason the army shells us."

Altogether I spent two weeks in the beleaguered town. Then it was time to get out. Latterly the bombardment from the hills had become even more intense. Once a fighter plane had roared over Zabadani and fired three rockets at a residential area. Unknown assailants had killed the president of the provisional town council. Abu Jaber feared that Assad's troops were about to overrun the town. "You'd better say goodbye to us and go, *habibi*," he advised. However, it was easier said than done. One of the smugglers who had brought me to Zabadani had been seized in a raid, and a rumour was circulating that his colleagues were thinking of offering me to the government troops as part of a swap. Abu Jaber was worried. "You're to be abducted, Christian. This is serious." From then on I wasn't allowed to stir out of his house, and armed men were posted at the entrance for protection. "But don't worry, we'll get you safely out of here," said Abu Jaber.

Just a few months' earlier journalists were thought of as allies and friends, a lifeline to the outside world which was beginning to lose interest in Syria. Things changed once the Islamists gained ascendancy in various parts of the country. In the simplistic view of al-Qaida and its friends, journalists are all Western spies, and infidels to boot. Criminal gangs see them as a way to earn big ransom money. Sometimes they are made into scapegoats on whom disappointed rebel groups can vent their fury at the inaction of the West. In November 2013 Islamic State fighters executed a foreign reporter, an Iraqi, in front of a television camera for the first time.

Three days of waiting. Three days filled with fear and uncertainty. Still Momin was protecting me and acting as my constant companion. Meanwhile Abu Jaber was bargaining with different smugglers, but nobody seemed willing to take the risk as the Syrian army was drawing its ring of steel ever tighter round Zabadani. "*Ma fi mushkila, ma fi mushkila,*" no problem, as Abu Jaber kept repeating like a mantra. His words were meant to soothe me but had the opposite effect. Then in the evening of the third day a delivery van stopped outside. "Quick!" cried Abu Jaber, "jump in, don't let anyone see!" Momin was there, ready to see me off. I pulled some crumpled dollar notes from my pocket, hoping to press them on Abu Jaber as a small compensation for having kept me in his house for two weeks, fed me and protected me. But no: "You're one of the family, brother. I don't want the money." The Islamist had spoken and that was that. We hugged each other. "*Inshallah*, you'll be in safety two hours from now!"

By this time, I knew what "two hours" probably meant. But the fib was well intentioned.

Chapter 8: Escape from Zabadani

There were already five rebels with Kalashnikovs in the back of the van; they were the armed escort for the expedition. Then there were the two smugglers who were to lead me over the mountains into Lebanon. And there were also five taciturn young men setting out to join their families in a refugee camp there. I was never to know their names as they refused to disclose them; the less we all knew about each other the better. Two of them could speak some English. One had been studying history in Damascus, the other had been running a grocery shop in Yabroud which he had taken over from his parents when they fled in the early days of the war; he had run out of goods and the Syrian army had come dangerously close so he had packed up and left. Both had but one aim: get out of Syria. Get to a refugee camp and safety; after that face whatever the future held.

We drove in the darkness along a track, sharing cigarettes and saying little. After a while the van stopped at the foot of a mountain whose slopes rose in front of us, shimmering in the moonlight. There we got down: the rest of the journey would have to be done on foot. All of us were reduced to one basic hope – that we might survive to see another day. For the risks were incalculable. In order to get through the ring of steel we would have to creep past dozens of checkpoints. Just two days ago a group of fugitives had been ambushed by the army; three of them had been shot and the rest taken prisoner. Only after much haggling and a fat payout had Abu Jaber been able to persuade the smugglers to take the risk of shepherding me out of town.

I can remember very little of the next two days. All I recall clearly is the fear. It was a fear which clouded every moment and every thought. I had ceased to be the professional journalist carrying out his research and documentation of everyday life in Syria; I was no longer a detached observer recording the flight of thousands in terror of bombs and fanatics; I had become a fugitive myself, a protagonist of my own story. Now, with no sense of direction and no plan, I wavered helplessly between hope and despair.

That first night we walked for nine hours. Just outside Zabadani we left the cart tracks behind and started climbing the steep mountain slope. Suddenly a blinding light enveloped us – a searchlight! We quickly hid behind a rock. Seconds later the silence was shattered by a rifle shot and a bullet whined into a jumble of rocks just metres away. My heart beat so hard I could scarcely breathe. One of the refugees buried his face in his hands and wept; others said silent prayers. Our escort fanned out, rifles at the ready.

I was paralysed by the fear of being discovered and shot by a Syrian army patrol. The smallest movement was torture for me. I could physically feel the fear as if it was a new part of my body; never had I experienced such intensity of feeling. I was wretchedly aware of being an encumbrance in our group whose presence further endangered the others. "Hold onto me," said the student from Damascus, dragging me uphill as I clung to his belt. The young grocer was propelling me from behind, another refugee was carrying my rucksack and one of the smugglers was taking care of my photography equipment. I felt ashamed at my weakness. They could easily have left me behind, or indeed bumped me off to save themselves trouble, I realized. Without me they would have been considerably safer.

Reaching the top of a mountain we stopped for a rest. The only bottle of water we had was passed around and we munched some biscuits. I was dehydrated and my tongue was sticking to my palate. The student patted me cheerfully on the back and smiled. A cold wind was blowing, but we gave each other a hug to counter the chill.

After a while a figure emerged from the darkness. It was a different smuggler, into whose hands we were now transferred. Our armed escort said goodbye and set off back to Zabadani. "*Yalla! Yalla!*" the new smuggler hissed in my year. Get going! Sharpish! Come on! His face was concealed in a balaclava. The sky was overcast and no moon was visible, so we had to make our way down the other side of the mountain in pitch darkness, tripping and stumbling as we went and getting cuts on our arms and knees. The new guide gave us no chance to stop for rests. Shortly before dawn we came to a small town which was under Syrian army control. "See those lights over there?" asked the student. "That's Lebanon. That's where we're heading."

So near yet so far. We hid in an orchard until a gang of men drove up on motorbikes. Everyone climbed aboard and the bikers took us to a safe house at the edge of the town which belonged to a Syrian family connected to rebel activists. Once again I could extract only the barest minimum of information. I was told that we'd have to spend the hours of daylight inside the house, out of sight of the occupying troops; and that at present it was too dangerous to cross the frontier as units of the Lebanese Hezbollah were on patrol there and had clashed with rebels the day before. A meal was served, then I lay down exhausted on a mattress. As I drifted off to sleep I could hear the sound of shots being fired.

I was impressed by the well-organized Syrian network of underground activists, smugglers and rebel fighters who incurred great risks in order to deliver their countrymen to refugee camps in Lebanon, Turkey, Jordan and Iraq. Of course they demanded some payment. But without such a network fugitives, especially young men who were not part of the armed resistance, would not have been able to leave Syria. The authorities would have seen them as potential rebels and imprisoned or killed them. The same routes as were employed to smuggle weapons, ammunition, provisions and fuel into Syria were used to spirit wounded fighters and refugees out of the country – and sometimes terrified journalists too.

We spent that day in the living room of the family of seven who were acting as our hosts. The lady of the house cooked for us, her husband spied out the neighbourhood on his motorcycle and used his radio to speak with rebel units monitoring possible escape routes. Two armed men had been posted at the entrance in case anyone had seen us in the night and betrayed our presence. At eleven o'clock in the evening a message was received saying the way was more or less clear: there were no new roadblocks, nor had the Syrian army made any new moves.

So we set off.

This was the most dangerous part of the journey. We had to get out of the town unobserved, then somehow manoeuvre around the checkpoints and avoid patrols. In this area there were no outcrops of rock to hide behind. I walked along, feeling strangely empty as I blindly followed the man in front. I couldn't understand anything that was being said, nor did I have any notion of what to expect. The history student was just behind me; he kept whispering "*Allahu akbar*" and pushing me gently forwards. We edged past houses, sticking close to the walls, then crawled on our stomachs across a field of vegetables, until at last we were out of the town. A pack of dogs picked up our scent as we crossed an open area, barking so loud I was sure they would give our presence away. We had to lie flat on the ground playing dead while the dogs sniffed at us; after an eternity they lost interest and trotted away again. Time got warped and events seemed to move both fast and slow. Our group had to keep stopping while the guides cocked their ears and listened. Every sound spelt possible danger – make a mistake and it could prove fatal. Life boiled down to that simple rule. On we crept, inch by inch, minute by minute. The Lebanese frontier was now only a couple of kilometres away.

At five o'clock in the morning we wriggled under a fence marking the border and crossed into the Lebanon, somewhere near the historic town of Baalbek. Safety was near. An ancient Mercedes was waiting for us and it took us into town. There we joined a family of Syrian refugees, eighteen people in all, who were living in tents on the flat roof of an apartment block. At last we could relax enough to turn around and embrace each other in relief. The tension of the past couple of days eased off; trembling and exhausted I sank to the floor. The student burst into tears; the grocer fell into the welcoming arms of his brother. Our guides started on their way back into Syria.

That same morning, I set off for Beirut. I was desperate to get home to my family as quickly as possible; and I was also keen to forget all about the preceding weeks of horror. I and my erstwhile companions parted ways, and I never learned what became of the others afterwards.

I had discovered what it was like to live in a beleaguered town and for a while I had shared the common fate of Syrian refugees with all its terror and uncertainty, indignation and helplessness. My experiences had traumatized me and altered me. For many Syrians the same experiences were the stuff of every day, and they had been enduring them for more than three years solid. On the flight home I wondered how Syrians would ever manage to get over the trauma of what they had lived through and return to some sort of normality.

Chapter 9: Calling Douma

Back home I received an email from Nermin, editor in chief of the Zabadani magazine *Oxygen*. She was letting me know that my friend Momin had been killed by a shell soon after my departure. I felt devastated, weak with horror, too shocked even to weep. Omar, the magazine's brave photographer, sent me a picture of the deceased Momin.

He looked as if he was asleep. His body was covered with a white sheet and only his face could be seen. I stared at the photo for hours. My memories were still so fresh. I remembered how we had walked through the ruined streets of Zabadani. Dear, loyal Momin, who had never left my side because he thought he could protect me with his presence. The little gifts he used to bring me, that kebab, the lukewarm cola. He had been a young man who refused to take up weapons and kill; instead he believed that peaceful resistance would ultimately bring freedom for his people.

In August Nermin wrote me a long letter. The Syrian regime had just sprayed some of the suburbs of Damascus with poison gas, killing over a thousand people. In her lengthy epistle she answered all the questions I had not asked when we were together and gave expression to the fury she felt at the way her revolution had been hijacked. "I'm finished. The resistance has now turned into a jihad. Yet once we had high hopes we could put an end to the regime by our own efforts," she wrote. "Which is worse, to die of poisoning or to be crushed by a tank? Or to be shot in the heart by a sniper or blown to bits by a rocket, or indeed tortured to death?" There was one passage I had to return to again and again, as it reflected the unbearable pain that brave young woman was having to bear. "I am a wife and a mother," she wrote, "and now work as a teacher. These days the main thing I have to attend to is the psychological welfare of my pupils. They are the children of war; they have all been affected by family tragedies. Some of them have themselves been imprisoned and tortured. I can't rid my own mind of the horror and I don't see how the children can save themselves from it either; how they can bear the daily racket of bombs and rifle fire or the constant fear of being tortured or killed. I still have my magazine and write in it about what it's like living in a climate of fear, but I am disappointed that the world just watches us die. They shouldn't do that, they shouldn't remain silent."

Oxygen was her safety valve, a way of channelling the horror so it wouldn't overflow and drown her finer feelings. She had used its seventy-four editions, one per week, to create a chronicle of the war. This despite the fact that she had no printer, no business know-how, no training in journalism. In spite of all the dangers and difficulties she had never thought of giving up. "The war against injustice will carry on, and we won't capitulate. We will fight against our enslavement and give expression to our thoughts and wishes. Yes, maybe when all's said and done the future lies in our own hands." That single thought is what enabled her to fight on.

On 29th August 2013, shortly after the poison gas incident, I got through to an eye-witness on Skype. Dr Ghazwan Bwidany was a slim man with a beard and spectacles, 27 years old, a medical doctor at the Syrian rebel stronghold of Douma. He spoke fluent English, having studied medicine in the USA for a few months and been in New York, Ohio and Michigan. He had witnessed the chemical attack on the Damascus suburbs on 21st August. He sat at his laptop ready for the interview, put on his earphones and apologized for the poor reception. Later on his electricity supply got cut off, interrupting our conversation. He started by smiling at the camera saying, "In these hard times we force ourselves to smile so as not to die of depression."

The events of that fatal August day were seared into his memory. The attack started at about two o'clock in the morning, he recalled. He was at home sleeping, as were most of his colleagues, when he received a call asking him to come at once to his place of work, a makeshift hospital called Maktab Tibbi Muahhad, which was about five kilometres from Zamalka, the central point of the chemical offensive. He thought it was just another of the usual kind of missile attacks they faced every day. Even when rumours about poison gas circulated he took no notice. Gas had actually been dropped previously, but only in the countryside where the population was low and few people had been affected. Since then everyone was afraid the same thing might be used in urban areas too. The inhabitants of East Ghouta had become panicky; if they smelt anything funny after a raid they would wrongly imagine they had been hit by poison gas. For that reason, Dr Bwidany did not at first listen to the rumours. "I honestly never believed Assad could be as stupid as to use poison."

At first no more than the odd victim or two appeared at the clinic, but they all had symptoms characteristic of gas poisoning: vomiting, foaming at the mouth, excess saliva, muscle cramps. He washed them with water and gave them atropine to counter the poison. But at about three a.m. all hell broke loose and patients started to flood in by minibus, lorry, van and even donkey cart. Often entire families had been hit. More and more arrived throughout the day and well into the evening. Not until ten o'clock the next morning had the chaos been brought under some sort of control.

Altogether ten doctors worked at his makeshift hospital. By the evening of that day eight hundred gas victims had been brought in for treatment, of which sixty-five had died, about a third of them children, though he didn't have the exact statistics with him. The clinic had been prepared for poison gas attacks but not on such a large scale. All available resources were soon exhausted: the atropine ran out and there was a shortage of ventilation equipment. Relatives of patients were asked to help with the nursing. "You don't have to be a doctor to treat these cases. All you have to do is wash them with water and give them oxygen. It's actually quite simple, but we weren't prepared for such a huge intake of patients. It was hardly something one could have foreseen. Of course we had catered for the possibility of gas attacks, which were not unprecedented. We had been training the nurses for months, and without them we couldn't have handled the situation."

"What were my feelings? I can scarcely remember. There was no time to think about them. It's difficult to put into words the things that go on inside you. I felt numbed and empty, I couldn't even weep. No, I wasn't afraid, there was no time for that either."

More victims had kept coming, from Zamalka, Erbin and Douma. The worst thing was dealing with the victims' relatives. "They were panic-stricken and wanted to know where so-and-so was, their mother, daughter, brother or whoever. They showed me photos and mentioned names. But we had no way of knowing the victims' names; many died in front of us and we could only record them as numbers. Even now some of the dead haven't been identified. Whole families were wiped out leaving nobody to identify them." He recalled a woman who had come to the hospital looking for her five children. All of them had been there, and all of them were dead.

Many of the children had died on their own while their parents were being treated. The doctor told me of a six-year-old boy who was still in intensive care suffering from respiratory failure. "We don't know whether he'll survive. But his whole family was killed in the attack." By now, he told me, most of the surviving patients had been discharged home, leaving only a few still under treatment like the six-year-old boy.

Days after the attack helpers were still finding bodies in houses; they had to break down doors to get at them. Whole areas of the suburb had been wiped out. Soberly, without emotion, the doctor told his tale and sometimes he smiled as if describing a family outing. Now and then shots could be heard in the background, but he never flinched. "Bullets are our daily bread," he said.

Dar' al-'asima, „shield for the capital city", was the name the Assad government had given to the vicious chemical assault.

Dr Bwidany was quite convinced in his own mind that it was the regime which carried out the poison gas campaign. "You think we'd do that to ourselves? To persuade America to help us? Myself, I'd rather die from Assad's bombs."

A further clue is that the Syrian army launched a missile offensive to follow up the chemical one. "For the last eight months we've had no electricity supply, we've been cut off, we're battered with shellfire every day, we've almost run out of food. At about seven in the morning, just an hour or two after the gas attack, the Syrian army launched an unusually intensive bombardment which went on until afternoon. They were trying to take over the districts we control. Many fighters had been killed in the chemical attack and we had to call for reinforcements from other parts of the city to stop the army from overrunning us. The FSA had destroyed about twenty tanks, that's why they attacked us with poison gas to weaken the FSA, break our resistance and take over our quarter."

One week after the attack Dr Bwidany met the UN inspectors, saw what they were doing and wondered what the point of it was. "It makes no sense. They're trying to establish whether poison gas was used, but not who used it. We already know gas was used, so they're not teaching us anything new. It's a waste of time."

The West had already made up its mind in any case. "There will be some minor reprisals against the regime, but that will be no help to us Syrians. That's just window dressing. The Western powers have no real intention of helping us. They've made many promises but nothing ever happens."

Dr Ghazwan Bwidany had given up hope of the West helping the rebels, he had lowered his expectations to a minimum. No half-hearted rocket attacks for appearance's sake; all he demanded was understanding. "Don't be afraid of us, don't fear Islam. Our ideology isn't dangerous. People in the West keep talking about terrorists and al-Qaida. Of course there are some extremist groups like Jabhat al-Nusra and Ahrar al-Sham, but we don't share their views and they are a small minority. The West is blinded by prejudice against Islam and ought to open its eyes to reality. Islamist groups control most of the liberated areas and they have put a stop to looting, theft and murder, which is what most people want. People like the Islamists precisely because they aren't extremists. We Muslims aren't enemies of the West, when will you realize that?"

Nevertheless, he agreed, the extremists presented a problem. "We have to protect minorities. For thousands of years we've lived together, Sunnis, Alawis, Shiites, Christians and Kurds. It must be like that again when the war is over. The extremists want an Islamic state, but we're going to prevent them." He admitted that atrocities had been committed against minority groups; the previous month extremists had attacked some Alawi villages and killed the inhabitants. "It's a big problem and it pains me," he averred.

Still, Dr Bwidany was confident that Assad would not win the war. He hoped the regime would be replaced by a political system which mirrored that of the USA while incorporating Syrian values, with laws that applied to everyone so that every individual could live his or her life freely in accordance with the rules. There was only one thing he feared, that there might be further poison gas attacks, for he was now convinced that Assad would use gas again.

Chapter 10: Chasing ghosts

My experiences in Zabadani had left such a profound impression I couldn't get away from them. Again and again I had nightmares about my traumatic escape, and each time I woke in terror before having reached the Lebanon. It was impossible to shake off that feeling of fear.

When I arrived back home after the Zabadani episode my wife collected me from the airport. She had planned a little surprise for me, a weekend with friends at a seaside villa; but what was supposed to be a dream holiday was for me a nightmare. I needed to be alone, I was not in a fit state to talk or answer people's well-meaning questions. How could I get them to understand?

The trauma would announce its presence quietly like some shy admirer, then gradually become noisier until finally it was screaming and yelling to be let out. For months I was numb and had no feelings at all, either positive or negative. Then suddenly I found myself questioning everything. I started having terrible doubts about my profession and about my marriage. Sometimes I cursed myself for being a failure and a lousy husband, other times I simply felt like chucking everything in and creeping away to die.

When we were desperately fleeing out of Zabadani we had walked through miles of grassland. The sharp awns of this mountain grass had broken off and stuck into my skin like miniature harpoons. And there they had remained; I had thousands of them all over me. I spent that weekend at the villa holed up in my bedroom with the curtains drawn, exchanging not a word with anybody, making use of the solitude to pull the little barbs out of my skin. Months later I was still finding odd ones in various parts of myself: my arm, my leg, my back, my heel, my palm, my calf. Each and every barb took me back to those two nights of trekking through the mountains along smugglers' trails in the direction of Lebanon. I felt the dogs sniffing around us as I lay prone; I was blinded by the Syrian army searchlight; I was suffocated by terror. In flashback I saw my comrades search for an escape route with a GPS device, their mounting anxiety, their panic when they thought they had fallen into an ambush.

People react to trauma in different ways. I did not wake up screaming in the middle of the night. I did not go berserk at the sound of fireworks. I did not sit in a corner trembling all the time. But my thoughts curdled and got bitter. Some traumatized journalists withdraw from the scene; others get more creative. I tried to find relief in new projects. I went to Egypt to meet a courageous activist striving for reconciliation and dialogue while the Muslim Brotherhood and the army tear the nation's soul apart in an atmosphere of negativity. I spent time with a man trying to change the way people think, an inspiring story. But my reporting failed to do justice to the drama of the events and the charisma of the protagonists.

One of the hardest things for me was to hang onto my inner conviction and integrity, my confidence in my own profession, at a time when the world suddenly felt poorer because something important had been lost, dissolved like a melting crystal. I found I had lost my impetus and my optimism. Worst of all I had started pitying myself. The same pictures kept revolving in my mind like a closed video loop. Again and again I recalled my moments of angst and went over the old scenes in review, what I had felt, what I had thought, and my emotions rose to a high. I wanted to carry on the fight alone, like a losing boxer who is knocked out each round but refuses to let his trainer throw in the towel. Eventually I decided to resume the fight with a new tactic.

As a journalist I was accustomed to slipping inside other people's skins in the course of my professional work. I felt the pain of a father whose son has been shot by a sniper, the despair of a woman who has been kidnapped by IS men and subjected to months of rape, the grief of a daughter coming across the bodies of her parents in a mass grave, the terror of a schoolchild whose school has been bombed, the anger of a soldier at the front line whose comrade is killed, the desolation of people who have nowhere to live but a graveyard. True, what had happened to them hadn't actually happened to me, but still their pain didn't just bounce off me like water on a duck's back. I needed to feel it in some depth if I was to relay their stories in such a way that people far away might get some idea of the truth. The sediment from such stories had gathered at the bottom of my mind like layer upon layer of toxic mud. It had become difficult to generate much interest in other things.

Probably that was a natural consequence of following a profession which often requited me to write about suffering and death. Previously I had happily shared my stories with anyone who would listen, and even some who were not so keen to hear them. I talked of Darfur, the Congo, Somalia, Afghanistan, Burma, Iraq. But now when I sat down with friends I would merely exchange a bit of small talk and crack a joke or two. If anyone asked about the situation in Syria I would answer with one word: awful. And then change the subject. It was unfair of me to discourage people who maybe genuinely wanted to learn, but I was too weary to describe the horror while off-duty.

I spoke of my problems to an acquaintance who worked at DART, an organization set up to help traumatized journalists. She referred me to a psychiatrist and we had a chat on Skype, or rather I talked while she listened. She told me I must get it all out of my system. "Talk to your wife, talk to friends, family, colleagues. The people around you need to know what you're going through." She warned me that my trauma would stay with me for the rest of my days; bones might heal but shattered souls did not. I had to face that and so did the other people in my life. Nevertheless, it was within my power to determine how much or how little the trauma should affect my daily activities. My will could assert itself and regain control, she told me. Her words encouraged me.

I resolved not to let my memories determine the course of my life, but small incidents taught me that although wounds heal with time the scars may go on hurting. There were still days when I was sucked back into the vortex of horror or felt a sudden sadness I could not explain. I found I could no longer go diving. As soon as I went underwater I had a panic attack and lost control. I avoided the claustrophobia of lifts, preferring to use the stairs. Some of my boundaries had to shift.

I had to try and knit together the torn sinews of my soul. If what my psychiatrist told me was true that process would never end. As with all life decisions, life had to be lived forwards but could only be understood backwards. I learned to manage my emotions. Henceforth awareness of my own vulnerability would help protect me. I learned how to accept difficult truths and so retain my mental integrity. At last I had no more flashbacks, no heightened pulse, no nightmares. With a smile I remembered a quotation from Dostoevsky: "Man can adjust to anything – swine that he is."

A few months later I got another email from Omar, the brave and loyal photographer of Ogygen, in Zabadani. Abu Jaber had died on 2nd January 2014.

Splinters from a shell had struck him just outside his home. He had promised his children he would go and visit them that day in the Lebanese refugee camp where they were; but he hadn't even got as far as his car. 2014 had started with the death of a man who had saved my life.

Chapter 11: Return to Aleppo, May 2014

The Islamic State had stepped onto the world stage. In June 2014 it declared a Caliphate extending from Syria into Iraq. The Syrian opposition struggled desperately against it in far-flung locations, in the process losing thousands of its fighters. At the same time the Syrian army seized its opportunity and created a blockade around Aleppo. Approach routes were cut so that no supplies could get through to its inhabitants.

Scarcely a day had passed since the end of December 2013 without the Syrian air force using barrel bombs on Aleppo. These were old oil drums packed with explosives and metal fragments which were lifted by helicopter and dropped on populated areas. That winter most of them had landed on schools, hospitals, blocks of flats and marketplaces, causing many casualties. The fourth year of the war had turned the once lively economic hub of Aleppo into a ghost city. In February 2014 the Security Council of the United Nations passed a resolution demanding an end to air raids on civilian areas in Syria, in particular the use of barrel bombs. The organization Human Rights Watch had proved with the aid of satellite imagery that at least 340 sites in Aleppo had been barrel bombed between December 2013 and February 2014. But nothing changed. Another organization, the Syrian Observatory for Human Rights, based in the UK, recorded 1963 civilians including 283 women and 567 children killed by barrel bombs in those three months alone. This indiscriminate massacre conducted by the Syrian army was driving the population out of the city and into refugee camps in neighbouring countries. Those who could not flee because they were too poor, too old or too stubborn had to barricade themselves in their homes.

Towards the end of April 2014 Syrian rebel forces managed, at the cost of hundreds of lives, to push the Islamic State fighters out of Aleppo and out of the villages on the Turkish border. They also re-captured the border crossing of Kilis, so establishing a corridor linking Aleppo to Turkey. My old friend Abu Yazan wrote to tell me that it was now relatively safe to visit Aleppo. An acquaintance put me in touch with a contact in Syria who said he was prepared to escort me there. In May 2014 I arrived at the Turkish-Syrian border.

Yosef, my contact, was waiting for me on the Syrian side of the crossing point Bab al-Salam. Aged 27, he was a short skinny fellow with a beard and a weary look in his eyes. Before the war he had been studying commerce in Damascus. Like many of his countrymen he had jumped at the chance to free Syria from its long-standing dictatorship. He took part in demonstrations and later fought against the forces of the regime as a member of a Kurdish unit.

Despair at the squabbling within the opposition combined with a love affair caused him to lay down his arms after a few months. He was now, in his own words, a media activist who posted material on Facebook and Twitter: photos and articles about the war, quotations from the Quran, cartoons ridiculing Assad and the followers of IS. In this way he hoped to keep reminding the world about Syria. Sometimes he took foreign journalists around Aleppo or up to the front and earned a few dollars as their general factotum. He was a man who had lost much hope but tried to make the best of his situation as a castaway of civil war.

We were in Yosef's battered Toyota heading for Aleppo. With us in the car was an armed escort of fighters of the Islamic Front, the main rebel faction in the area at that moment; four young men whose job was to make sure I reached Aleppo in one piece and was not abducted on the way – like Steven Sotloff a few months before. Steven, a US citizen, had hired Yosef as his interpreter, and while we drove along Yosef described how the hijacking incident had taken place.

On the morning of 4th August 2013 Steven Sotloff climbed into Yosef's vehicle at the Turkish-Syrian frontier. Yosef was going to be his driver cum interpreter, a risky job as at that time foreign reporters were being abducted by Islamists on regular basis. But Sotloff needed material for a story, Yosef needed the money. The cost of living had recently risen five-fold and few job opportunities existed in Aleppo after three years of civil war. If Yosef didn't go for it Sotloff would employ someone else. Yosef had been monitoring the approach roads to Aleppo for days, looking out for bandits and Islamist road blocks, and thought he had the situation sized up.

He had had a bodyguard of three armed men with him when he picked up the American journalist, but they were no match for the soldiers of ISIS. The journey came to an abrupt halt at Marea, about forty kilometres north of Aleppo. Armed men stopped the car, pulled Yosef and Sotloff out of it, blindfolded them and with several blows from their rifle butts shoved them into a waiting vehicle. "Someone had grassed. The IS men knew when and where we were meeting up, which route I had chosen and which kind of car I drove," Yosef told me. His captors took him somewhere, he had no idea where, and shut him in a cellar. Masked men interrogated him several times a day. They were non-Syrians, people from Tunisia or Morocco, and they demanded why Yosef had been working for an infidel. He was lucky; after fifteen days they let him go, just like that. But what had happened to Steven Sotloff he did not know. There was a rumour that he was still being held in an IS prison somewhere, maybe in Aleppo, maybe in Raqqa, but no trace of him had been surfaced since then.

By the time Yosef had finished his tale we were in Aleppo. He drove through the destroyed city, steering past the ruins of a former hospital. Dr Othman, the head doctor of Dar al-Shifa whom I had interviewed during my first visit in 2012, had had to flee because he had dared to have a black IS flag removed from the hospital entrance and was consequently threatened with execution. After three years of war and over 190,000 casualties the Arab Spring had turned into the Syrian Winter. The United Nations High Commission for Refugees counted 2.8 million refugees and 6.5 million internally displaced persons; that meant almost half the total population of Syria was on the run. And the tally was increasing day by day.

The IS fanatics exploited the circumstances of chaos to wipe out anyone opposed to them. An alliance of Syrian rebels had managed to expel them from Aleppo, but now they were on the move again and were taking over the smaller towns and villages around the city. "I'm a Muslim," said Yosef, "yet the IS call me an infidel because I don't share their world view. They are murderers with warped minds, distorting everything into black and white, *halal* and *haram*, good and evil."

Hundreds, even thousands of Syrians had already fallen foul of IS ideology. "They shot a fifteen-year-old boy in front of his own mother because they thought he had insulted the Prophet," growled Yosef. Summary execution for supposed blasphemy was carried out then and there, in the street: several shots in the head. In Raqqa, the Islamic State's main stronghold, individuals who stood in the way of the extremists were being shot and crucified regularly: academics, journalists, moderate revolutionaries, Shiites, Kurds, anyone with different beliefs. The IS posted pictures of their dead bodies on social media.

Yet Yosef was not ready to leave his homeland and flee to Turkey. "How could I leave my own country in the lurch? That would make me feel like a traitor," he declared, lighting a Gitanes cigarette and inhaling the smoke.

I could hardly recognize Aleppo. Our drive took us past bullet-ridden cars and ruined houses. Yosef kept a loaded pistol lying on the ledge over his dashboard. "Just a deterrent," he explained, flicking the butt of his cigarette out of the open window. Again and again we had to stop and run for shelter in ruined buildings as helicopters circled or fighter jets roared over. The few citizens around also took shelter and watched the planes. "Soon the bombs will start falling," said Yosef uneasily.

An elderly grocer waved his hand, inviting us and some others into his shop. "It's safer inside," he said, then disappeared into a back room, to return with freshly brewed black tea and a *nargileh* or hookah. "Syrian hospitality!" smiled Yosef. "That's something even Assad's bombs can't destroy." While waiting for the missiles to rain down we all sipped tea, passed the water pipe around and made rude jokes about President Bashar al-Assad. Two barrel bombs exploded a few streets away, then the local men said goodbye and went on their way as if the air raid had just been a penalty break in a match. Yosef wanted to get moving too. A couple of hundred metres from his car a plume of smoke was rising into the summer sky.

Death had long been a part of Yosef's life. He often passed through the sights of a sniper's rifle or saw bombs and shells explode nearby. He watched friends die. He also observed how the people of Aleppo were drawn together by adversity. That was something Yosef wanted to show me.

After a forty-minute drive he parked his car outside a block where a friend of his lived. The friend operated a sort of underground kitchen, where he and three assistants cooked meals and served them free of charge to hundreds of hungry inhabitants of front line areas. Yosef and his friend discussed current problems with supplies. The friend said he hadn't been able to serve any meals for the past five days as his area had been under constant air attack.

Later Yosef stopped outside a former school in the Bustan al-Qasr district. There we found pathologist Abu Jaffer, 55, a thin man with deep set eyes, standing over the partly decomposed corpse of a man. "Welcome to the house of the unknown dead," he said, stroking his grey beard with one hand and with the other holding his nose against the sickly smell of rotting flesh. "We found this man yesterday in an abandoned building." His assistant took a photograph of the body and recorded its gender in his register. The name and age columns of the form were left empty. Then he manoeuvred the corpse into a grey body sack and zipped it up.

On the tiled floor of another room lay a body which had lain unclaimed at the war front for several days. Abu Jaffer made a note in his book. "We keep records of all the dead people whose bodies no-one has recovered in case relatives come looking for them," he explained, and pointed at the wall where hundreds of photographs of mutilated bodies were on display. Not a day went by without anonymous corpses being brought to the school. Sometimes fifty arrived in one day, sometimes only one. The previous year, Abu Jaffer told me, the bodies of more than two hundred men and boys had been recovered from the Queiq river. Many had their hands tied behind their backs and a shot wound in the head. From time to time the pathologist's voice broke and he dissolved into tears, then painfully pulled himself together and resumed his narrative. He was sick to the teeth with the war, he admitted. Just then a married couple came to the door, searching for a missing relative. With a mixture of hope and dread they started scanning the photos on the wall.

Yosef said goodbye to Abu Jaffer and we left the morgue. As we did so another barrel bomb fell. "Oh, it's a long way away," muttered Yosef, shrugging his shoulders and driving on regardless. We passed more ruined houses, piles of rubble and burned out cars.

Yosef had an appointment with Umm Modar, the headmistress of a secret school in Salaheddine district.

The school was at the end of a side street, hidden behind the high walls of an apartment block. We found the 32-year old headmistress sitting in her makeshift office, where she apologized for the mess. "The army has been targeting our schools," she explained, "so we had to move into a private dwelling." As she spoke she kept drumming her fingers on the sheet of glass covering her desktop. Umm Modar was a plump woman and despite the heat had her hair hidden under a canary yellow headscarf and blue robes swathing her body down to ground level, for she was a strict Muslim. She said it was hardly possible now to keep any classes going. Most of the teachers had fled and parents were anyway afraid to send their children to school because of the general insecurity. Still, in her view it was important to carry on in spite of the bombs, rockets and sharpshooters. Not least on account of the two dozen schoolchildren aged six to thirteen who were sitting in the next room eagerly awaiting their teacher.

"Children, which of you have experienced an air raid?" asked Umm Modar. Twenty-four hands shot up.

"And who has lost a relative in the war?"

Eight-year-old Faisan put up his hand and announced in his piping voice that his father had been shot by a sniper. Nine-year-old Nur went through a list of war victims: her uncle, her sister, her grandfather. "Can I include more distant relatives and friends?" she concluded. Umm Modar smiled at her and shook her head. Fatima, ten years old, put up her hand and told the class she had been present when her grandfather had been killed. She held up a picture she had drawn, showing two tearful hearts pierced by swords. "I'm not going to cry," she said, trying to choke back her tears as she wiped her eyes. "We're going to take revenge and kill our enemies, God help us!"

Yosef was sitting at one of the desks, flopped back and stifling a yawn. Then suddenly he roused himself as if something had alarmed him and sprang to his feet. We had been at the school for a whole hour, much too long. He needed to get home, but first he had to keep a promise to visit a certain friend. He said goodbye to the teacher and waved to the children, and off we went. Twenty minutes later we were in the Saif al-Dawla quarter. Yosef stopped his car outside a shabby block hidden among a maze of back streets. The two upper storeys had been destroyed by bombardment. Yosef knocked on an iron door, then descended a spiral staircase leading to the basement. In it was one of Aleppo's numerous underground kitchens in which volunteer helpers prepared food for fellow citizens who would not otherwise get enough to eat. Sufficient foodstuffs were still on sale in the shops but many people could not afford to purchase all they needed as prices had risen by over five hundred percent over the past two years.

Yosef was engulfed in hot steamy air as he entered the kitchen. In a pantry three men were squatting on the floor beside a mountain of onions and garlic which they were chopping small and tossing into a big pan. Packets of macaroni and tins of cooking oil were stacked in a corner. In the next section stood a fat man stirring noodles in a cauldron with the help of a long wooden spoon and wiping the sweat from his brow with a handkerchief. "*Salam alaikum*, Yosef," cried another man. "Feeling hungry?" Yosef thanked him and excused himself, saying his wife was already waiting with his supper and would be cross if he was late. The men laughed heartily and shook their heads. "You don't know my wife!" protested Yosef.

Soon the manager of the kitchen, Abu Khaled, appeared on the scene. He and Yosef embraced, then sat on the concrete floor, drank sugared tea from tiny glasses and discussed the situation in Aleppo. Abu Khaled explained that his team hadn't been able to dish out any food for the past five days because helicopters kept dropping barrel bombs on the district. "One bomb hit our building, but down here we're quite safe, praise God." Today was the first time they had once again ventured out with food to distribute. While the two were talking Abu Khaled's men were filling six large containers with noodles in thin sauce which were then carried upstairs. A couple of dozen children were at the entrance waiting with empty pots and dishes. "We haven't had anything to eat for days," said a girl with a small sister in tow who was crying. A veiled woman cloaked in a black robe got busy doling out the food with a ladle, portion by portion, child by child, laughing and joking with the children as she did so. When she ran out of food and there were still children queueing outside, begging for something to eat, tears came to her eyes. "I haven't got anything left, darling. Please come back tomorrow. I'm so sorry, darling." She had to repeat the same sad message to each child and kept brushing the tears away and shaking her head as she watched the youngsters go back home empty handed.

Yosef had to get going too: his pregnant wife was waiting for him with the supper. "She always gets terribly worried if I'm late arriving home," he explained.

I spent my first few nights with Yosef and his wife Amira in their flat in one of the back streets of Sheikh Maqsood, the Kurdish quarter of Aleppo. Yosef had more or less given up any hope that the madness would come to an end. He stood in the street outside his house, tipping his head back and squinting at the bright sky, listening to a rumbling sound which gradually grew louder as if it was a thunderstorm brewing in the distance. Then he spotted the fighter plane. The Syrian air force had been bombing Aleppo since early morning. Yosef looked for somewhere to hide, kneeled behind a rusting car and watched the silver blip in the sky as it came nearer, moved away again, curved sharply, turned and then hurtled towards the city like a bird of prey closing in on its prey. After firing its rockets, it climbed high again. The whole process was repeated, accompanied by the chatter of the rebels' anti-aircraft guns.

While Yosef watched the attack from the street his wife Amira came out on the balcony of their fifth floor flat and peered anxiously down. "Yosef, where are the bombs falling? Will they attack our area?" She stroked her stomach; she was now in the eighth month of her pregnancy. A smile stole over Yosef's face when he saw her. "They're falling not far from here, darling, but don't worry. Go back inside now. I'll be back for supper." He got into his Toyota, laid his video camera on the back seat and set off. He was taking me somewhere I urgently had to go. I was to meet the people who were the main reason for my coming to Aleppo: the White Helmets.

Chapter 12: The White Helmets

The White Helmets were a kind of civil defence
brigade made up of about a hundred volunteers.
They were unarmed civilians and their task was to
move in after each air raid, rescue people trapped
under ruins, take care of the injured and recover dead
bodies. They were firemen, rescue workers and
paramedics all in one. They were financed by
international charities, mainly Islamic relief agencies
from Europe, USA and the Middle East. Since the
Syrian military had started bombing villages and small
towns around Aleppo and in other provinces
additional White Helmet units had been set up there
too.

The White Helmets were part of a growing
minority of younger generation revolutionaries.
Instead of shooting at people they undertook civil
duties and helped order the chaos. In Aleppo
electricity and water supplies had been cut off, refuse
collections had ceased, there were shortages of
doctors, medicines and food. Hospitals and schools
had been destroyed. Normal life was impossible, but
people like Khaled Hajo were trying to fill some of
the gaps left by war.

Khaled was the director of the White Helmets in
Aleppo. I met him in the courtyard of his operational
base in the Hanano district where he and his
colleague Ahmed were sitting on plastic chairs. He
was wondering how many deaths they would witness

that day, how many people they might save. A Syrian helicopter circled overhead; Khaled and Ahmed craned their heads to scan the sky. Ahmed, nicknamed al-Tawil, the long one, because he was as tall and thin as a stick of sugarcane, was puffing heavily on his cigarette, as if hoping to dispel the agitation he always felt when helicopters flew over. All around were ruins: shattered walls pocked with bullet holes, houses with collapsed upper storeys, mounds of rubble, burnt out shops.

"Do you think he's going to attack, Khaled?" asked the tall one, pointing to a blob in the sky which was glinting in the morning sunlight.

"Hmm," mused Khaled, screwing up his eyes to see better.

The headquarters of the White Helmets was a former vehicle pound belonging to the traffic police department of the Syrian administration. A couple of Toyotas which had never been reclaimed by their owners were rusting away in the yard. Two men stood guard at the gate, keeping their eyes on the sky. Constant danger had drawn strangers together. In between air raids they would sit in one of the two rooms which served as base, common room and bedroom. A number of dirty mattresses lay on the floor, a television set stood in one corner, a ceiling fan churned the warm air. Electric current was supplied by a generator.

The helicopter was still circling overhead like a malevolent insect. "He's sure to attack," said Khaled.

The only question was where the barrel bombs would fall and what they would hit. Maybe Sakhur district would be targeted, or maybe Tariq al-Bab or the Shaar area. Or this very spot. It wouldn't have been the first time.

As the two men watched the helicopter tilted slightly, then a black object tumbled out of its side door and plummeted earthwards. The sky was filled with a humming sound as if a swarm of angry hornets was coming down to attack.

"Barrel bomb!" shouted Khaled, flinging himself to the ground. Seconds later a deafening boom rent the air and a great mushroom of dust, smoke and rubble billowed up. "Fuck you, Bashar!" cursed the tall one, making a rude gesture at the sky.

"A second bomb is sure to follow," said Khaled. "We'll wait for it, then get on our way," He looked at his watch: eight a.m.

Khaled Hajo, the quiet, charismatic White Helmets boss, thirty years of age, had been a lawyer before the war. He had been one of the first volunteers who came together in early 2013 when the regime started battering residential areas of Aleppo with rockets. At first nobody had thought of setting up a brigade for recovering bomb victims. Only when the Syrian military began using this new weapon to spread terror and sap resistance to Assad's regime did the loose band of volunteer helpers organize themselves into a disciplined rescue service.

Five minutes after dropping the first bomb the helicopter returned, circled once and dropped a second barrel on exactly the same spot. "Take cover!" cried Khaled, and everyone took shelter behind walls or lay flat on the ground. Chunks of masonry and bomb metal came rattling down on the yard. "They always do that," said Khaled. The aggressor's tactic was both evil and effective. After the first explosion shocked residents would come rushing out and helpers would make their way to the scene. Then the helicopter would return and drop a second bomb on them. "That way they can kill more people," Khaled explained drily. He chewed his lip as he scanned the sky.

When Khaled gave the order to start his men ran over the road and squeezed themselves into two fire engines, which were parked under a tree so the air force pilots couldn't see them. At top speed, with sirens blaring, the vehicles charged through the desolate landscape, past ruined houses with jagged steel rods sticking out of them and tattered curtains flapping at empty windows. As they raced along some of the volunteers kept their heads out of the windows scanning the sky for fighter planes and helicopters. The brigade might well be targeted by planes or snipers while out on an operation, Khaled told me; such a thing had happened before, as the bullet holes in the windscreen testified. The fire engines were heading for the pillar of smoke which was gradually dispersing.

On the way Khaled told me about the training the White Helmets were given. It was provided at a location well away from the front and took two weeks. The programme was filled with classes on such things as assessing war damage, giving transfusions, providing first aid, driving fire engines and cutting through concrete and steel to release trapped people. At the end of their training the volunteers would receive a pat on the back, be given their uniform and equipment and immediately go to work where the bombs fell. "*Your house is on fire, we'll put it out; if you want us, just give us a shout!*" chanted Ahmed and his fellow rescue workers from the rear seats, clapping their hands in rhythm as they sang

It was only a matter of minutes after the second bomb had fallen that the first team reached the road in the Shaar district where it had landed. The bomb had ripped balconies off buildings, shattered windows, cracked walls and crumpled cars as if they had been made of card. A heavy silence lay over the street; a pale ray of sunlight stabbed through the clouds of dust. On the ground lay all the scattered stones and pieces of masonry which had rained down from the sky. Figures were emerging from the chaos, mere shadows, staggering and coughing, amazed to find themselves alive. A lifeless leg was sticking out from under a pile of rubble.

Khaled, al-Tawil and his mate Alaa, a Turkish paramedic, rushed to and fro across the road like manic puppets, jumping over ruined walls, vanishing into a black hole where once a door had been. There they found an eleven-year-old boy lying with a gash in his head, a bone in his shattered left forearm poking out, blood oozing from his mouth. His father was standing beside him in shock, weeping and then cursing the helicopter pilot and the president. Khaled quietly gave orders, suppressing the feeling of panic which gripped him at such moments. The important thing was not to lose control. Oh yes, somebody must be told watch out in case the helicopter returned. Al-Tawil led the father out of the building, taking him by the arm, to save him from the sight of his son.

Alaa lifted the boy's limp form and carried him in his arms to a side street where he laid him carefully down on the pavement. He checked for any sign of a pulse, shook his head, wiped his bloodied hands on his overall. "Just look," he cried in anguish, pointing at the overall, "this is the blood of an innocent child!" The boy was clearly dead. Khaled placed a sheet over his body and then put his arm round Alaa, holding him tightly until the young volunteer had calmed down.

Then al-Tawil questioned the local people to find out if anyone was buried under rubble or missing. Alaa and other volunteers looked for severed body parts, for according to Muslim belief each body should be complete when buried, ready for the Day of Judgment; the dead person would suffer if any part was missing. The volunteers carefully recovered lost limbs from the ruins.

While Khaled's team searched for body parts the local inhabitants started to resume their lives. They looked through the holes that had been blown in their walls, shook dust from their hair, called to each other to see if anyone was hurt or missing, called for help, threw broken possessions out of their windows. A paramedic appealed for people to donate blood as the hospitals were running out of supplies.

Suddenly someone shouted *"Tayyara! Tayyara!* Aircraft!" A helicopter was circling over the neighbourhood. "Out of here! Quick! *Yalla, yalla, yalla!"* yelled Khaled. Then the hum of a falling bomb could be heard. "Twenty seconds," whispered Khaled. His face was distorted with tension and fear. His lips moved, counting the seconds: one, two, three...

Twenty seconds was the length of time between the release of a bomb and its detonation. With luck it might explode far away. If it fell near you nothing would make any difference. No wall would be enough to protect you, the heat of the explosion would deprive you of oxygen, the blast would rip open your lungs, your sinews, your entrails.

While residents sought refuge in the ruins of their houses the barrel bomb burst in a different area several hundred metres away. The rescue team raced back to their vehicles and drove back to headquarters at top speed. Their first sortie had clocked three dead, five seriously injured.

Fourteen more barrel bombs fell before lunchtime. Most hit buildings which were already empty. Shortly after ten a.m. an MIG fighter plane fired two rockets into a market place in Tariq al-Bab. A father and son shopping for vegetables were killed. As the White Helmets placed the bodies on the back of a lorry a barrel bomb landed two streets away, wounding an old man and ripping another man to shreds.

Khaled was the only person in his family to stay back in Aleppo. The others had long ago fled to reception camps in Turkey. For nine months he had been living at the headquarters of his Civil Defence Force, and during that time he hadn't taken a single day off. He was a pensive man but not a cold one. Given the right circumstances he would gladly marry, have a family and return to work as a lawyer. "But which woman would marry a man who could be killed any moment?" he asked with a wry smile, lighting a cigarette with the butt of the previous one.

Khaled was the man in charge. There was only one rule his men were obliged to follow: try and stay alive, don't play the hero, for bravado can prove fatal. "Save yourself so you can save others," as Khaled put it. He repeated it many times like a mantra. But words are sometimes vain.

9th March 2013 had started like any other. In the night fighter planes had roared over. When the sun rose the helicopters had come and dropped their barrels of explosives in foray after foray. All as normal. Volunteers Ammar, 20 years old, Ihab, 22, and Ahmed, just past his eighteenth birthday, had set out as usual too that day. But something was different, though they had no way of knowing it: the bombers had changed their tactics. After the first bomb had been dropped the helicopter remained hovering in the air until the rescue team arrived. "The second bomb hit them while they were pulling members of a family out of their burning car," said Khaled, beginning to weep at the memory. As well as his volunteers seven local people and a Canadian journalist were also killed. Since then Khaled and his team had never gone out until after the second bomb had fallen.

His deceased colleagues sometimes appeared to Khaled in his dreams as if to tell him it wasn't his fault that they had died. But it was he who had sent them on that operation, and he himself had not gone with them because he had been feeling exhausted from the previous night's activities. There was no escape from his feelings of guilt. Maybe he could have averted the disaster if he'd been there, maybe not, but the question remained. *"Huw al-aleem"*, God knows. They buried the three friends in an old football ground near their base "so they're near to us."

Soberly Khaled spoke of the daily horrors he went through; sometimes he broke off and stayed silent for several minutes before wearily resuming his story. He talked of battered corpses, people torn to shreds, smothered children. There was that three-year-old girl they had recently pulled alive from the ruins of a building after she had lain buried for hours; despite their efforts she had died in hospital the following day. There was that family they had pulled out of a wrecked flat, all fourteen of them, every one of them dead. He kept hearing in his mind the desperate cries for help, growing gradually weaker when he and his team were unable to reach them in time.

Every day he had to re-set his mental clock, conquer his fear, repel all the images of horror. Occasionally, when he felt he could stand the war and the pain no longer, he had a moment of weakness and wondered whether a falling missile, death from on high, might not actually be a merciful relief for him, a way to end it all.

Afternoons were usually relatively quiet. 20-year old Ahmed, the tall one as they called him, had lost hope of surviving the war. He would sit on a bedstead sucking at a hookah and using Facebook and WhatsApp to communicate with his girlfriend. She lived in the government-controlled part of Aleppo, only a kilometre or two away yet quite out of reach. He hadn't seen her for eighteen months. The civil war had not only divided the city, it had separated many loved ones from each other. Ahmed had dreamed of becoming a fireman like his father since

he was a child. "Thanks to Assad that dream became
a reality," he commented bitterly. But it was hardly a
decent existence. "There's nothing in Aleppo. We
have no electricity, no water, no future. Only bombs.
We're doomed to die. Fuck you, Bashar!" He
sounded more helpless than angry.

While al-Tawil flirted with his girlfriend on his
smartphone or updated his status on Facebook his
companions would doze the hours away, sing along
to Jennifer Lopez songs or dance to the tune of
Gentleman, a hit by Korean artiste Psy. Like any other
young men, they liked to fool about, crack jokes, chat
about football and girls or discuss what they were
hoping to study after the war.

Al-Tawil's best friend was 25-year old Alaa Sharif,
a Turk, who as soon as the Syrian war broke out had
quit his studies in Istanbul, said goodbye to his
parents and hastened to the war zone to serve as a
paramedic. He was a pious young man who rejected
violence. He often quoted from the Quran and his
decision to risk his life at a war in another country
was based on its teachings. "Whoever kills a human it
is as if he had killed all mankind, and whoever saves
one it is as if he had saved all mankind," he quoted
(surah 5 verse 32). He practised his kindness by
feeding Lulu, a cat traumatized by all the bombing,
which had taken refuge with the White Helmets.

Lying on the floor beside him Ahmed Mursi
stared at the ceiling fan above his head. He was a shy
twenty-year-old with a bushy mop of hair who had

deserted from the Syrian army because he was unwilling to shoot at his own countrymen. He had joined the rebels to fight against Assad, but again hadn't been able to stomach the killing. Finally, he had found his niche in the White Helmets. "I want to save lives, not destroy them," he said. With each bomb victim they pulled from the ruins they regained another chunk of the self-respect which the war had taken from them. That work kept them going and gave their lives some direction whilst their country was mired in confusion.

Al-Tawil's view was somewhat more pragmatic. "It gives you a buzz. People love us, they clap and cheer when we drive past. I love this job," he said chuckling. He enjoyed being a hero. He took his iPhone and sent his girlfriend a selfie showing him in the process of saving a girl. Under the photo he wrote *habibi*, my loved one. In the evening the Free Aleppo TV channel aired a report on the White Helmets. When they saw themselves on the screen and heard the presenter call them heroes they bent double with laughter, then argued about which of them looked the coolest.

At moments like that Khaled, their leader, kept in the background. He sat in his own corner with his laptop on his knees, watching his men and smiling quietly like a proud father, though in fact he was only a few years older than them. He poured himself some black tea to banish the tiredness, lit a cigarette and turned on the shortwave radio he used for listening in on the government troops. One pilot was telling another he had loaded some barrel bombs at their base and was now about to drop them somewhere in the city. Khaled shrugged his shoulders, it was nothing unusual, his days were invariably punctuated by regular barrel bomb blasts.

Night was the worst time. Hanano was right on the war front, next to the government-controlled zone. Every night fighter jets would roar over the White Helmet base, shells and rockets would rain down on the neighbourhood. Tracer bullets fired by the anti-aircraft gunners would glimmer in the night sky, debris would rattle down on the roof whenever there was an explosion close by. Then I would push myself right up against the wall and cover myself with the mattress in the futile hope it might afford some protection. When morning came I would wake up feeling knackered. As usual Ahmed would bring me a cup of tea and greet me saying, "Welcome to paradise!"

In the al-Sukari district on 16th June hundreds of hungry people were queueing for a free meal when two barrel bombs were dropped on them. More than sixty civilians died – just as the World Cup was opening in Rio.

I had already spent too much time in Aleppo. I had intended to stay only five days, a quick in and out, taking no unnecessary risks. Now ten days had passed. Once a car stopped beside me and two armed men jumped out. "Who are you? What are you doing here?" they wanted to know. This is it, you're about to be abducted, I thought to myself. Serve you right. Just then the tall one came running up to explain to the gunmen who I was and what I was doing. "*Ma fi mushkila*, no problem!" The men then offered me a cigarette and we sat on the kerb smoking. My heart was pounding, but all was well.

Some days I had experienced as many as twenty-five or thirty barrel bombings before lunchtime. I had seen the barrels being thrown from helicopters. Minutes later I had visited the spots where they had exploded. I had seen dismembered children, wounded women, dead men – not just once or twice but every day. The areas targeted were almost always residential ones. Once a hospital was bombed. Another time I witnessed a fighter plane fire two rockets into a market and saw a shell-shocked boy walking around with a severed arm in his hand. There had been no armed rebels in the neighbourhood. I never ventured to the front where conventional government troops and rebels faced each other from their trenches; it was just too dangerous. It would be virtually unfeasible to report from those locations; working in such conditions was extremely difficult, verging on impossible. It took time and one needed to have helpers on the spot, people one could trust who knew their way around, had good contacts, could "read" the war and knew where the front line was and how things were changing over time. People like Yosef, Khaled, Alaa or Ahmed. They were lifesavers.

Towards the end of July 2014 over seven hundred Syrians died in the fighting in the course of two days. Still, in among all the fear and horror there were moments of joy in Aleppo too. In August Yosef's son was born. Yosef and Amira named him Bakr after the Prophet Muhammad's father in law. Meanwhile the Syrian army was tightening its hold on Aleppo. The industrial area of Sheikh Najar came under its control and the rebels' supply lines were cut. "It is only a matter of time until the city is taken over," wrote Yosef in despair. "We are threatened with the same fate as Homs."

At the same time in the area around Aleppo the IS were taking over one village after another and advancing ever closer to the city. That was enough to shake Yosef's obstinate determination to stay put in his homeland. "I now have a responsibility for my son, it's no longer just about me," he wrote at the end of August. "I'm quitting." He was ready to go anywhere else. The revolution for which he had risked his life had been snatched from his grasp. There was too much hatred, dissent and envy among the rebels, who now were often fighting each other. "We're no better than the regime. There's a bit of Bashar in all of us. The dictator has won the day."

Khaled, the tall one and many more of the White Helmets fled to Turkey. There had been a dispute with the municipal authorities, and it centred on money. Khaled had insisted that the families of White Helmet workers killed in action should continue to receive their wage of a hundred dollars a month, to enable them to survive. The town council was unwilling to foot the bill. Khaled and his men held demonstrations in the streets, their demands were discussed on TV, then a rumour went around that they were all gay – effectively a death sentence. And so they quit.

Chapter 13: Calling ISIS

For weeks IS had been dominating the headlines.
The war in Syria had spread into neighbouring Iraq.
The very thing the international community with its
policy of non-interference had hoped to avoid was
coming into being. In Syria the IS besieged the
Kurdish town of Kobane. Observers feared that a
massacre of the Kurdish population was imminent.
In Iraq Islamists murdered thousands of people
belonging to the Yazidi minority. With my son Leon
asleep in my arms I kept close track of the news.

Syria had become a no man's land, a minefield for
foreign journalists, so from that point onwards I
chose to concentrate on the battle against Islamic
State. The war in Syria was inseparably bound up
with the war in Iraq. Anyone who hadn't followed
what had been going on in Syria for the previous few
years would never be able to understand how IS had
risen to become the world's most powerful terrorist
group; how with the help of its trademark method of
stirring up fear it had swiftly gained control of Manbij,
Yarablus, Deir Ezzor and Raqqa in Syria and Tikrit,
Ramadi, Falluja and Mosul in Iraq; how in 2014 ten
thousand Iraqi troops could be put to flight by a few
hundred IS fighters who rode into each town on
pickup trucks, firing wildly, drove out the Christians
and murdered the Shiites and Yazidis. By raiding
banks in Mosul the IS got their hands on hundreds of
millions of dollars, enough to fill up their war coffers.

With the armaments they stole from Iraqi arsenals they managed to overrun a region the size of Great Britain and subdue the Sunni tribes in it.

I tried to contact IS fighters. I was looking for people who had been in IS ranks and would tell me about the Islamists' world view and the way their caliphate was supposed to work. I wanted to try and understand. After much searching I at last found a man who was ready to talk.

On 15th September 2015 I got hooked up to this man on Skype. He was in a hiding place some-where in Turkey. His camera showed a small apartment with bare walls. I saw my correspondent, who gave his name as Abu Alkakaa, move rapidly across the room, then sit down on a brown settee. At that point he chose to switch off the camera, so from then on I received nothing but his soft, high pitched voice.

Abu Alkakaa had been in hiding in that flat, which belonged to an acquaintance of his, for ten days. Where exactly in Turkey it was, he would not say. Nor did he want to show his face or tell me his real name. Abu Alkakaa was a *nom de guerre* he had assumed in honour of a radical preacher of that same name who had been murdered in Aleppo in 2007. He now wanted to remain anonymous not only to elude the Turkish authorities but also to stay safe from the IS agents who were actively seeking new recruits all over Turkey.

There were quite a few young men around claiming to have left the service of the Islamic State who were keen to sell their stories to the Western media. Often they were shameless exhibitionists ready to embroider and dramatize their tales to impress the journalists. For example, there was a Norwegian Islamist who had fought for a couple of months under the Islamic State in Syria but at the time in question was working at a kindergarten in Oslo. He was asking fifty thousand Norwegian Krona for his inside story. I made a decision neither to give money to potential terrorists nor to offer them a forum for their propaganda.

Abu Alkakaa did not want money, all he wanted was to talk, while preserving his anonymity. Our interview had to be postponed twice for security reasons. Several reliable informants in Syria and Turkey had recommended him to me, and they also confirmed the truth of what he told me.

Abu Alkakaa told his story calmly and thoughtfully without rancour. He felt no need to make excuses for himself because he had no misgivings. He gave a sober account of the inner workings of the Islamic State. As he talked children could be heard playing and laughing in the background.

He came from a moderate Sunni background and was studying chemistry in Damascus when the civil war broke out in 2011. After a few months, rebels had taken over whole regions and the regime led by Bashar al-Assad had largely lost control. Salafists, long suppressed and persecuted in Syria, moved in to fill the political vacuum. While various other opposition groups were fighting for a democratic society radical preachers called for young believers to battle against secularism.

Abu Alkakaa was one of those who heeded their call. He abandoned his studies, went back to his home town of Deir Ezzor and joined a small local Salafist group. Their aim was to set up an Islamic state founded on Quranic principles with the Sharia as law. Making temporary alliances with some of the rebel bands they fought Assad's troops as best they could with their limited equipment, setting ambushes and so on. The Syrian air force was meanwhile bombing Deir Ezzor into a desert.

The scales tipped in the radicals' favour when Jabhat al-Nusra, an offshoot of al-Qaida with roots in Iraq, entered the stage of the Syrian civil war. It had everything the Syrian rebel groups did not: modern weapons, plenty of ammunition, money, discipline, unity. It had financial support from rich Arab and Sunni sources, and it had experienced soldiers, chiefly from Chechnya, Kosovo and Iraq. Abu Alkakaa's unit merged with Jabhat al-Nusra and from then on fought under the black flag of al-Qaida.

Thousands of rebels from other groups also joined al-Nusra. Many of them were moderates who had simply become exasperated with the fragmentation and inefficiency of the moderate opposition. They overran one village after another and drove the government troops out of their bases.

Soon al-Nusra was in control of significant parts of the country and even conquered the city of Raqqa.

In August 2013 Abu Alkakaa joined a group which split from al-Qaida and called itself the Islamic State of Iraq and the Levant (ISIL). He felt at home with its ideology, which was if anything more radical even that that of Jabhat al-Nusra. Its adherents fought in the name of God to establish a caliphate with the Sharia as its law. They were prepared to kill anyone who stood in their way – and there were plenty who did stand in their way.

For two months Abu Alkakaa served in a unit charged with enforcement of the Sharia in the towns and villages ISIL had taken over. He was one of the numerous morality wardens on patrol, looking out for anyone improperly dressed, listening to music or consuming alcohol. Anyone who broke the Islamic moral code was punished. Abu Alkakaa said he had flogged people but never executed anyone. More complicated cases were brought before a Sharia judge. Abu Alkakaa knew of many instances where the death sentence had been passed; in his view the offenders deserved to die because they had not behaved like true Muslims. In Raqqa, Aleppo, Hasaka and Deir Ezzor he had seen people strung up to die on lampposts and scaffolding. Executions took place in a public place; the condemned individuals would be beheaded or shot. The victims might be moderate Muslims, academics, journalists or activists. Thieves would have their hands cut off. Abu Alkakaa had thought such punishments were fair and belonged to a world order it was worth fighting and dying for. His dream then was to die a martyr and go to heaven.

Before long the IS were pitting themselves not only against Assad's troops but also against the Free Syrian Army and other rebel groups. Abu Alkakaa despised the rebels and their desire for a secular democratic government. He thought their ideas would corrupt the Islamic vision. Man could not place himself above God's laws; true Muslims obeyed the word of God and acknowledged no other rule; there was no place in the Islamic State for unbelievers. Shiites and Alawis were not real Muslims. Anyone who opposed the caliphate had to be eliminated, and that included any Sunnis who fought against IS. None of them should be spared. "God willing I would even kill my own brother if he was fighting with the FSA against IS." Christians, Yazidis and adherents of other religions would be allowed to live in Syria, for Islam was tolerant and just, but they would have to pay the traditional protection tax or else convert to Islam.

After two months as a morality warden Abu Alkakaa had been sent to a training camp on the Iraqi border. For forty days he had learned how to drive a tank and fire rockets. At that time increasing numbers of foreign volunteers were joining the IS: people from Chechnya, Kosovo, Britain, Germany, Australia, France, Saudi Arabia. The civil war in Syria had become a global jihad. The IS conquered Mosul,

Kirkuk and Falluja in Iraq, Bab, Maara and Deir Ezzor in Syria. Abu Alkakaa confirmed that thousands of Iraqi soldiers had been executed; they were Shiites and thus enemies of Islam who had been killing Muslims. He thought more should have been killed.

On 29th June 2014 his dream became reality: Abu Bakr al-Baghdadi, the head of ISIL, declared a caliphate with himself as caliph. Abu Alkakaa and his fellow soldiers swore eternal allegiance to their leader. ISIL was renamed ISIS (Islamic State of Iraq and Syria), or simply IS (Islamic State).

Not long after that Abu Alkakaa had his first niggling doubts: not about the basic concept of an Islamic empire but about the methods being used to achieve it. In early August that year IS troops overran his native province of Deir Ezzor. One day 370 people were killed, another day 220; Abu Alkakaa himself was involved in the killing. After the battles were over he saw unarmed civilians being shot and beheaded; he watched the shooting of women who attempted to shield husbands condemned to die. Killing an enemy in war was permissible in Islam, said Abu Alkakaa, but slaughtering an unarmed person or a woman was *haram*, not permitted, and it counted as murder. The execution of foreign hostages was also wrong when they hadn't actually been fighting against the Islamic State. Abu Alkakaa did not wish to have deeds like those on his conscience, though at that stage he still hesitated to make his misgivings public.

Very quickly he learned that it was safer to keep his views to himself. In early September 2014 a Jordanian fighter in Abu Alkakaa's unit complained to an officer about the frequent executions of defenceless civilians, which he said went against the principles of Islam. Next day the objector's corpse was discovered lying in a back street.

In Abu Alkakaa's view chopping off the hands of thieves and flogging women who didn't veil themselves properly was all right; putting Shiites, Alawis and infidels to death was justifiable. But when he saw his fellow soldiers executing unarmed civilians in his home province even he thought things had gone too far. One hot summer day he made a decision: he would quit.

From then on the 26-year old spent all his time brooding on how he could safely take leave from his post on the Syrian-Iraqi front. He thought of possible ploys and excuses, tried them out in his mind, rejected them. Lying went against his conscience because it was *haram*. It would be wrong to deceive men he had trusted as brothers and comrades in arms.

One thing was clear: if his erstwhile comrades found out that he'd lost conviction or got wind of his plans they would kill him. The Islamic State demanded unquestioning loyalty. But, thought Abu Alkakaa, my loyalty is to God alone.

In that case he would have to run away.

He had planned his exit carefully. If he was found out he would be tried as a traitor and certainly condemned to death. Then he would be shot, or beheaded, or nailed to a cross as many had been before him. He had secretly obtained a fake permit and planned to travel to Turkey, the only place he could hide. To reach his goal he would have to pass through territory held by the Free Syrian Army. He managed to cross the enemy zone in the back of a lorry. At each checkpoint he showed his false pass and hoped not to be found out – if his identity had become known he would have been shot straight away. But he was in luck. After three days he crept through a hole in the fence separating Syria from Turkey. He then got onto a bus and went into hiding. He believed, his god had protected him.

Now there was no way he could return to Syria; it would have been suicide. He said he would gladly re-enter the war against Assad and fight for the caliphate, but not using the methods of the IS. When mentioning the IS he sounded like a man who has been dumped by a beautiful lover: wounded, bitter, disappointed and angry. He said maybe he would join in a jihad somewhere else; it didn't matter where, the enemies of Allah were everywhere.

My attempt to understand the IS via a Skype interview did not satisfy me. To know what was really happening, or at least get some idea of it, one needed to be on the spot. In November 2014 I flew to northern Iraq. My goal was Sinjar, a city beleaguered by IS. A couple of months earlier I had read an article on the internet telling how the Kurdish-German Kasim Shesho, from Bad Oeynhausen, was commanding a brigade of three hundred men in the Yazidi pilgrimage town of Sherfeddin and desperately trying to hold off an overwhelming force of Islamist fighters operating under the name of Islamic State of Iraq and Syria (ISIS). ISIS had just taken over northern Iraq in a matter of weeks and was engaged in a massacre of the Yazidi population in the Sinjar mountains. Yazidi men were killed, the women abducted, the children enslaved. Helping Shesho were his son Yassir and his nephew Haydar. They were defending the one last town in the Sinjar range which hadn't yet fallen into ISIS hands. Yazidis from Germany were pitted against ISIS extremists.

Chapter 14: Sherfeddin, November 2014

It was no easy matter to get to Sherfeddin. At the end of November, I reached a dreary town called Zakho on the Iraqi border. For days I waited for permission to join one of the relief flights the Iraqi air force was operating twice a day to bring food, water, weapons and ammunition to the trapped Yazidis on Mount Sinjar. When at last I got permission freak weather arrived. Mist and rain held up the flights, then an extra sortie had to be mounted against an ISIS position. *"Bukra, inshallah,"* General Ahmed, commander of the air arm, would say every morning. He was a wiry man wearing an air force uniform and reflective sunglasses. Tomorrow, God willing.

For five days God was not willing. While waiting I visited a town called Rabia on the Syrian frontier; beyond it stretched the caliphate. A Kurdish post there had been attacked by ISIS that morning. Several suicide bombers had blown themselves up, taking the lives of thirteen Kurdish Peshmerga with them. I walked past the remains of the assailants not long afterwards. An arm was sticking up from a mound of earth, part of a leg lay in the grass. Peshmerga fighters were posing for photos beside the bodies like big game hunters with their trophy. I counted eight ISIS corpses with their long beards, tousled hair and youthful faces. My sympathy for them was limited. They had caused much suffering and killed people who were my friends and colleagues. But nor could I join the Peshmerga in their joy over their deaths. What a waste of life was all I could think, looking at the dismembered bodies. What twisted logic had led those young men to blow themselves to pieces and cause as much additional carnage as they could. 'Suicide bombers', that was a silly, bland and misleading term; 'murderers' would be more appropriate.

The morning of the sixth day brought clear blue sky and bright sunshine. General Ahmed was waiting for me on the airstrip; he was in a good mood. "You'll be flying with me, and I've never yet had a crash," he said smiling, giving me a pinch on the left cheek. "The first helicopter over there is my one. Just chuck your things in the back." As I put my bulletproof jacket, photography kit and rucksack in the hold I secretly hoped this wouldn't be the day he had his first crash. Before we set off I phoned General Shesho to tell him I was on my way. "Very good, son. I'll send someone to pick you up."

We took off. Sitting in the open doorway on either side of the craft was a guard armed with a machine gun. General Ahmed turned to me, grinning to reveal a perfect set of white teeth, and gave a thumbs-up. I nodded. Fine, I thought as we flew over northern Iraq, or rather over the caliphate of the Islamic State. When the helicopter landed on a road on top of Mount Sinjar fifty minutes later chaos ensued. Hundreds of desperate people rushed up to it and the other aircraft, jostling against the open doors, pushing, shoving and calling out. There were Kurdish Peshmerga fighters, wounded people on stretchers, refugees with grey fearful faces. All of them wanted to get off the mountain, where there had been a severe food shortage for months and people had been having to sleep in tents in sub-zero temperatures. An old woman was sitting weeping on a boulder with a thin blanket around her shoulders; her feet, without socks, were in plastic sandals. A father begged a pilot at least to take his children to safety. Uniformed men with sticks were trying to control the crowd, whacking heads, arms and backs with their staffs. When the helicopters took off again one young man tried unsuccessfully to cling onto the undercarriage of one of them. I observed the scene in alarm and wondered how I was ever going to get away again from this dreadful spot.

I made another phone call to Kasim Shesho, the Yazidi general from Germany. "Oh, you are here already?" he asked in broken German, sounding surprised. Then he passed me over to his son Yassir. "So you're here already?" repeated Yassir. Then he told me to find somewhere to sleep for tonight on the mountain top; someone would come and pick me up next morning. By this time thick clouds had covered the mountain, rain was falling and an icy wind was blowing. I knocked on the door of a temporary servicemen's camp belonging to PKK, the Kurdish Workers' Party, introduced myself politely and was allowed in. A very young woman, maybe seventeen years old, who was wearing battledress and carrying a Kalashnikov, gave me a friendly nod, showed me to an empty mattress and handed me a bowl of lentil soup. That evening I fell asleep, exhausted, surrounded by fifteen chain smoking fighters who were watching Turkish cloak and dagger films on an old television set with the volume turned right up. Each time the hero knocked out a villain they clapped in delight and broke out in song, rendering verses from Kurdish patriotic songs.

When I woke next morning, 21st November, Hassan was standing by my mattress. He was a man past middle age with grey hair and a kind smile. He explained that General Shesho had sent him to fetch me, but it took some time for the message to get across as he knew no English and I no Kurdish. We exchanged smiles and I followed him. For four hours we stumbled down steep mountain slopes covered in stones, stopping now and then to smoke a cigarette and share a bar of chocolate. Standing on an outcrop Hassan stretched out his arm and pointed to a small group of buildings at the foot of the mountains. "Kasim Shesho," he said. Then his finger swung very slightly further north. "*Da'ish*," he said. "Islamic State." He uttered that name in a tone of disgust as if it had a foul taste, and made a grimace with his mouth. My eyes moved from one of the points he had indicated to the other and gulped. It was hard to gauge distances, but Shesho's base could not have

been more than a thousand metres from the ISIS one.
We must already be within range of their snipers'
rifles; two figures on a bare mountainside, we could
easily be spotted with binoculars. As we neared the
foot of the mountain Hassan moved ever faster, and
the final hundred metres were a downhill sprint.
"*Da'ish*, bang bang!" explained Hassan graphically.

A camouflaged Toyota Hilux was waiting in a low
lying area, and from it stepped Kasim Shesho and his
son Yassir to receive me. "Welcome to liberated
Kurdistan," growled Shesho in his thick gravelly
voice. He was a quiet 62-year old man in
camouflaged battledress with a fleshy face and bald
forehead; his eyes were hidden behind thick
sunglasses. His voice was deep and he had the
throaty cough of a chain smoker. When walking he
dragged his left leg, damaged in a road accident years
ago. He was the chieftain of the largest and most
powerful Yazidi clan, the Yoana. His people spoke of
him respectfully as the 'Lion of Sinjar' or 'Lord of the
Mountain',

A ten-minute drive took us into Sherfeddin, the
pilgrimage town. General Shesho apologized for not
being able to offer me any hospitality. "We have little
to eat," his son explained. "Our last food delivery
was two weeks ago. We're running out of supplies
and ammunition."

In my first four days in Sherfeddin nothing
happened at all. Time passed with difficulty, minute
by minute, hour by hour. Sometimes I walked around

the pilgrimage sites, accompanied the Sheshos to the temple or visited the trenches where weary fighters were whiling away the long hours.

Electricity was strictly rationed. A generator was turned on for two hours a day so that the fighters could recharge their mobile phones and radios and get a chance to check the results in the European football league tables. At night Sherfeddin was a dark hole in the landscape, with only the moon to spread some silver light over it. The inhabitants were forbidden to light lamps in case they offered a target to ISIS rockets and shells. By six o'clock everything was pitch dark and most of the fighters crept into their sleeping bags and were soon snoring. Only Kasim Shesho remained sitting awake in the flickering light of a candle, drinking sweet tea, smoking non-stop. Every couple of hours he would go up onto the roof to give encouragement to his lookouts and snipers there. During these long nights the Yazidi general filled me in on the previous chapters of his life.

Kasim Shesho knew all about warfare. As a young man back in the seventies he had been here in the Sinjar mountains with other Kurds fighting against Saddam Hussein. He had been captured, imprisoned and tortured. On his release he had fled first to Syria, then to Germany where he had claimed asylum. He settled in Bad Oeynhausen in the province of North Rhein Westfalia and in due course acquired German citizenship. After the fall of Saddam Hussein in 2003 he had divided his time between Bad Oeynhausen, where he did odd jobs as a gardener, and the Sinjar mountains, where local people kissed his hand as a lord. He said he had received much kindness from Germany, but Iraq was still his real home.

The Shesho family had been living in Bad Oeynhausen for 26 years. Kasim's children had all passed their school leaving exams, done their military service, found employment and started their own families; their life in Germany was settled and unremarkable. Kasim had imagined that his fighting days were over. Until, that is, ISIS overran his homeland.

When the ISIS attacks began in August 2014 Shesho happened to be on a visit to Iraq. He stayed on and rallied his fellow veterans of the war against Saddam Hussein: old men with grey beards wearing the traditional Arab *kufiya* as their headdress, who smoked roll-ups made with newspaper. To start with there were only a few dozens of them and all the equipment they had was some rusty Kalashnikovs left over from previous wars, but gradually more men joined Shesho's militia. Many expatriate Yazidis came back from abroad, particularly from Germany. One such was Ali Layen, who three months earlier had left his wife and seven children behind in Hanover to come and join the war. "Kasim Shesho asked for help and we answered his call," he said, stroking his stomach. "He is our leader." Abu Layen always wore a fur cap and sunglasses. Another man, who was from Wolfsburg, liked to hail me in German every time he saw me. "Wie geht's? Alles klar?" How's things? Everything OK? Brilliant! As ISIS moved ever nearer the Kurdish government eventually supplied Shesho's army with modern armaments: machine guns, shells, bazookas and so on.

It was an odd little company Shesho had drawn up against the well-equipped ISIS force. There was a mixture of grisled old men and young striplings. Elderly men showed boys the age of their grandsons how to fire a bazooka and taught them to keep their nerve when the enemy attacked. A generation for whom war was a thing of the past and another for whom it was something they had merely heard about were now fighting side by side.

Sometimes a supply helicopter belonging to the Iraqi authorities would drop off food, water and ammunition. Shesho claimed to have enough men, weapons and ammunition to defend Sherfeddin. But for that very reason he was at loggerheads with the other Yazidi clan chiefs. They were bitter because Shesho was better equipped than they were, yet was only mounting a defensive operation. In response Shesho growled that if he were to move troops forward to attack that would leave gaps in his defences and leave the town vulnerable. He also pointed out that the ISIS had planted mines to stop his side from advancing and he had no mine disposal teams to deal with that problem. Shesho was a man of few words and when he did speak it was about the conduct of the war. Ammunition was already running low, he said with an apologetic gesture. "If only we had more men and more weapons, then we could attack and drive ISIS out."

That didn't look likely. The Iraqi army had as yet made no appearance. There was no trusting the Kurdish Peshmerga: as soon as ISIS had come on the scene they had upped sticks and run away, leaving the Yazidis exposed; nobody had forgotten that. The last weapons delivery from the Kurdish government had been quite a while back. The Yazidis were on their own. "As always," commented Yassir. So the Sheshos had launched an appeal for funds. "One hundred percent of your donation will be passed on," Yassir promised on Facebook, earning a paltry 67 Likes.

Things weren't easy for the General. His men at the front were waiting for him to advance. And about a kilometre beyond Sherfeddin forty cold and hungry families, mostly dependants of the front line fighters, were living in wind battered tents. Old men and women, wives and children, they were too proud, too poor, too obstinate or too exhausted to flee. As the Lion of Sinjar Kasim Shesho had to try to please everybody. If he visited the refugees in the hills for whom he was responsible his fighters would complain he was avoiding danger. If he lingered too long at the front the refugees would say he was indifferent to their plight. It was like tightrope walking. As he couldn't be in two places at the same time his son sometimes stood in for him. Yassir was his father's adjutant, confidant and bodyguard rolled into one. "My father is elderly and I'm here to support him," he said, speaking with a regional German accent. Yassir was also the militia's press officer, taking the war into German living rooms via the social network media. On Facebook he posted photographs, updates, news briefings and sometimes a video of his father discouraging his Muslim neighbours from joining ISIS and appealing for their help in fighting the extremists. One clip was viewed over thirty thousand times.

He felt proud of his responsible role, Yassir said, but he would much rather be a hundred and fifty metres down the road, fighting alongside his cousin Haydar whenever an attack was launched by the "ISIS swine" as he called them. Yassir, who held a German passport, had in fact received basic military training in the German army, but his father had not wanted him to fight. Yassir had to beg him for permission to accompany him to Iraq.

Yassir Kasim Khalaf, 26 years old, who had worked in a catering firm when at home, had been in Sherfeddin since the beginning of September and he was slowly getting used to the situation. "Of course I was scared stiff at first. In this place you never know what's going on." But after the first few clashes one understood more or less how things worked. The periods of inactivity were the hardest to bear: all that waiting for the next onslaught, the constant suspense, the uncertainty. The only certain thing was that enemies were lying in wait a few hundred metres away and all they wanted to do was kill you for your religion. "Bonkers, isn't it?" So far they had managed to fend off each assault by ISIS. But they were coming steadily closer, and one had a nasty feeling that the rest of the world was leaving the Yazidis in the lurch. Another bad thing was the food: beans morning, noon and night, sometimes with rice, sometimes with couscous, sometimes with dry flatbread. Reserves of drinking water were also running low and the pump motor had just broken down. "After a time you get used to the fact that nothing is right here," said Yassir, tossing his cigarette butt away. ISIS had more than once tried to send suicide bombers disguised as Yazidis into the garrison with the aim of assassinating his father. "They were tried by the clan elders and sentenced to death," Yassir said flatly. "Such people aren't humans, they're barbarians."

Yassir never spoke to me about his family back home in Westphalia. But he phoned them every evening if a connection was available. "Hello. How are things? Everything all right? Yes, yes, everything's fine here, don't worry. That's it, right, yes." He did not wish to add to the anxieties of his dear ones. A few months earlier he had been in tranquil Bad Oeynhausen watching the TV news with his relatives in the living room of their home. For days on end

they would hear nothing from his father, brothers
and cousins in Iraq. "One week we did nothing but
cry," he recalled, pressing his thumbs into the corner
of his eyes. He took a deep breath and continued.
Days after that they had learned that Yassir's younger
brother Fahim had fallen into the hands of ISIS;
luckily he had somehow escaped with his life. At that
point Yassir made his decision: he must join his
father.

Yassir intended to return to Germany only when
ISIS had been defeated. Until then he would stay at
his father's side. And after that? He had no idea. He
would have to get used to ordinary life again, life
without danger. He already had little contact with his
former friends. "What could I talk to them about?
They could never imagine what it's like here. Maybe
they think my reports are just bullshit, though I
expect there are some who go, Wow, crazy stuff,
man!"

Naturally he was missing Germany, and most of
all he missed his family and a proper bed. "But we've
got no choice. Are we to sit back and watch while
our people are slaughtered and our temples
destroyed? Never. If ISIS took over Sherfeddin that
would spell the end for Yazidis in Iraq. We'd rather
die on the spot." Too many people had died already.

The Islamists viewed the Yazidis as idol
worshippers because they revered fire, a peacock
figure and various angels. The Yazidis were in fact a
secretive community whose members would only

marry among themselves within the framework of a complex caste system. They kept themselves to themselves, not least because again and again over the centuries they had been persecuted, killed and driven from their homes. "This is the seventy-fourth episode of genocide against Yazidis," Yassir remarked.

My conversations with Yassir and his father interrupted the boredom of endless waiting. Much of the time I lay shivering in my sleeping bag and stared at the ceiling. Then one foggy December morning the ISIS army advanced on the Yazidis in five armoured Humvees.

It was just before eight in the morning, a Wednesday. Mist as thick as cotton wool covered Sherfeddin. As soon as he looked out of the window Yassir knew something unpleasant would happen. "Shit!" he cursed, lighting a cigarette. "ISIS weather."

Yassir smoothed his uniform, shoved a magazine into his storm rifle and slung the rifle over his shoulder. He picked up his smartphone and posted a status update on Facebook. "!! URGENT !! If we're not slaughtered by ISIS we're going to die of hunger and/or cold – unless help arrives sharpish!" The post got 365 Likes.

Yassir sat down beside his father on the sofa where the latter was talking to a couple of officers of his militia. The officers, elderly men in uniform, scratched their grey beards and slapped their thighs with laughter whenever one of them cracked a joke. I went up the stairs onto the roof of the building and surveyed the thick white soup Sherfeddin was drowned in. I could see no further than twenty metres. Even the closest buildings were only faintly visible in the mist. I lit a cigarette and while I was smoking a humming sound suddenly rose out of the fog. It was coming nearer; it was the noise of a vehicle approaching.

The sun struggled to pierce the fog with its rays like a weak searchlight. A diffuse light was cast on the pilgrimage town of Sherfeddin. In the centre of town the pointed steeples of the temple could be seen sticking out of the mist. Sherfeddin is the second most holy site of the Yazidis, coming after Lalish, the spiritual centre of the secretive sect, which is sixty kilometres north of Mosul. Yazidi defence positions were located on the hills all around the town, armed with mortars, heavy machine guns and bazookas. Lookouts hidden behind walls and in trenches kept their binoculars trained on the ISIS positions day and night. Everyone, that morning, was ready for action. Yazidi fighters patrolled the streets, Kalashnikovs at the ready, fingers on the trigger, eyes screwed as they peered into the murk. Sharpshooters were positioned on the roofs all round. A rabble of dogs raced down the street, making the soldiers jump. "Listen!" said one militiaman, putting his hand to his ear. The drone of a vehicle motor could be heard in the distance. Another of the fighters cursed the fog

which made it hard to gauge where the vehicle was;
the only certain thing was that it was rapidly getting
nearer. "Those arseholes always attack when there's
fog," said Yassir.

At that instant the assault began. 8:30 a.m. Shells
flew overhead and landed in the old cemetery beside
the temple. Bullets whizzed through the air. Yassir
and I ducked behind a wall; my temples were
throbbing. From their positions the Yazidi defenders
shot at the approaching Islamists. Yassir ran back
into the building where his father was. I stayed put
behind the wall and watched a shepherd and his
family fleeing uphill away from the firing; a girl was
screaming in her father's arms. General Kasim
Shesho stood on the veranda outside the hall which
had once been a place of assembly for Yazidi
pilgrims but was now his headquarters; its thick walls
would protect the occupants from shelling. Shesho
kept talking into his phone. Was there enough
ammunition? Were the sharpshooters ready? From
which direction was the attack coming? He sent men
with bazookas and ammunition to strengthen the
gunning positions, then went up on the roof,
crouched down behind a wall and through his
binoculars studied the arid plain streaked with dried
up watercourses which lay below. He detected some
ISIS soldiers hiding near a radio mast. A shell
exploded just behind him but he hardly flinched.
Then a messenger came to tell him that the enemy
had moved right up to the edge of the town, scarcely

a hundred metres from headquarters. They were using five armoured vehicles for the attack. Shesho asked whether anyone had been wounded or killed. No, said the man, not on our side, but two ISIS men had been hit. Shesho gave a shrug, nodded to dismiss the messenger, then glanced at his watch. Nine a.m. Outside more shells were exploding and shots were being fired.

The previous October ISIS had started a major offensive, moving to within a few hundred metres of Shesho's defences. Since then the holy town of Sherfeddin had remained encircled by ISIS, their gun positions easily visible. Three hundred Yazidis faced several thousand ISIS troops. Sometimes when night fell the ISIS men would be a kilometre away, then next morning only eight hundred metres would separate the two sides. On a mountainside local people had laid out stones to spell a desperate message: HELP US.

Even when there was no ISIS the area was a difficult one to live in. Midsummer temperatures reached fifty Celsius; in winter icy winds scoured the region and rain turned the ground into a morass. According to Yassir hundreds of Yazidis had died of cold and hunger that winter, hundreds more had been killed in fighting or executed. An unknown number had been buried in mass graves. Thousands had fled into the mountains where they were now living under canvas in temporary refugee camps, waiting to be rescued from the cold. They had no electricity and no drinking water. Their only lifeline to the world was the air link: twice a day, weather permitting, two rickety Iraqi air force helicopters came to deliver supplies and take away a handful of refugees.

It was 9:15. The din of gunfire echoed loudly from the mountains all round. I followed a group of militiamen carrying bazookas and ammunition to the front line. There, behind a protective wall which ringed his compound, stood Haydar Shesho, the general's nephew. The fighters next to him were firing shots at some retreating ISIS soldiers. "The Islamists drove towards us in five armoured Humvees," Haydar explained, his face radiant. The barrel of his machine gun was hot from firing. In the compound his men were rejoicing at their victory, raising their weapons in the air, slapping each other on the back and praising Taus-i-Melek, the angel in the form of a peacock which Yazidis worship. "*Hol hol'a Taus-i-Melek'a! Hol hol'a Taus-i-Melek'a!*" they cried in unison. Haydar pointed to some tyre marks on the ground in front of his base. "That's how close they came, hardly fifteen metres from us." Some skull fragments and bits of brain tissue were lying in a pool of blood on the asphalt. One of the militiamen spat in disdain at these human remains. A shell whistled in and burst on a hillock nearby; the men took no notice but I got a fright and flung myself to the ground. It was now 9:30 and the battle was over.

Soon afterwards Kasim Shesho and Yassir came along. They both embraced Haydar. The clan chief congratulated him on having successfully repelled the attack and Haydar told him how the battle had been won. Noticing the fragments of skull Kasim Shesho pulled a blue plastic bag from his trouser pocket, bent down to pick up a piece of bone with the tips of his fingers and put the bone in his bag as a trophy. Yassir took a photograph. This photo showing the blue plastic bag was later posted on Facebook. Yassir knew that the ISIS people followed his posts. The photo got 460 Likes.

Meanwhile Kasim was talking on his mobile phone to an official in the Kurdish government, asking for supplies. "We urgently need new munitions. We may be able to hold off another one or two attacks but no more." He lit a cigarette and inhaled deeply. His phone kept on ringing; the news of the ISIS assault had spread rapidly. Other clan leaders rang to offer their help; friends rang to ask how he was. And then an interpreter speaking on behalf of the American alliance came on the line, asking whether any air support was needed. Shesho rolled his eyes and said thanks, the battle was over now, but some air raids on ISIS positions would certainly do no harm.

Within a short time, USAF jet fighters came roaring over Sherfeddin. General Shesho stood on the roof of his headquarters giving instructions to the pilots over his mobile phone. With the aid of coordinates and descriptions he clarified where the ISIS was entrenched and where its armoured vehicles were. Yassir was filming him as he did so. The American planes flew low and thundered over the town, then black columns of smoke rose from the dismal plain. "That's it, the swine have had their lot for today," rejoiced Yassir as he folded up his camera. "Pity the air raids always come when it's too late." He shook his head and watched the smoke disperse in the wind. The time was then 10:30 a.m.

"It was a close call. They've never before come as close as that," exclaimed Yassir when we were all back in the operations room relaxing on a sofa. A hundred or so fighters had gathered to celebrate their victory; they were singing, clapping their hands, taking photos of each other and of themselves. Too close a call, Yassir's father was thinking. That afternoon a small lorry drove up. General Shesho took me to one side and told me I really must get out. ISIS would soon launch another attack and this time they might breach the Yazidi lines. Although he didn't say as much I could guess that he viewed a German reporter as an added liability, an unwanted burden – and a valuable prize for the ISIS if they caught me. "The ISIS have known all along that you're here," Yassir told me. "It just isn't safe enough to stay."

Luckily, I didn't have to climb back up to the helicopter landing pad on top of Mount Sinjar.

Kasim Shesho had provided a vehicle for my escape. But the weather was foul and the mountains were veiled in clouds. I was held up for eight days, during which time I stayed with some PKK fighters in their grimy camp. There were about three dozen of them and they kindly shared their food and their cigarettes with me.

When I got home I found an email from Yassir in my inbox. "What use is a life of ease if your father, brother, cousins, family, relatives, friends, clan, tribe, religion and country are all fighting for survival? None at all! That's why I'm staying here. We shall either prevail together or die together, here in our Sinjar mountains. *Hol hol'a Taus-i-Melek'a, hol hol'a Sherfeddin'a!*"

Chapter 15: Sinjar, April 2015

A few weeks after my visit to Sherfeddin an alliance of Kurdish Peshmerga from the banned Kurdish Workers' Party or PKK plus fighters from the Syrian defence union YPG pushed ISIS out of much of northern Iraq and took over part of the Yazidi capital, Sinjar. That marked a turning point in the war against the Islamic State. In April 2015 I travelled to the region again. My goal was get into the still besieged city of Sinjar which the PKK was defending from ISIS.

The road to Sinjar was a dangerous one. We made for the holes which the Kurds' January offensive had punched in the ISIS lines, a sort of corridor through the caliphate. For hours we drove along empty roads and through deserted Kurdish villages occupied until recently by ISIS. We were stopped at one checkpoint after another and had to show passports and visas and explain that we were journalists heading for Sinjar. A Peshmerga fighter at one checkpoint shook his head disbelievingly. Sinjar? That's still in the hands of *Da'ish*!

The word *Da'ish* spread terror in people's hearts despite the fact that ISIS had recently been pushed back, suffering considerable losses and forfeiting yet more of their supposed invulnerability with every battle they lost, every village the Kurds took over from them. They had lost Kobane, a Syrian town which the Kurds had triumphantly snatched back from them after months of bitter conflict and many deaths. They had lost Tikrit, birthplace of the Iraqi dictator Saddam Hussein, which had been taken over by the Iraqi army with the help of Shiite militias in early April.

Now Sinjar was due for liberation. It had the same symbolic significance for the Yazidis in Iraq as Kobane did for the Kurds in Syria, as a key prize in the fight against *Da'ish*. For four months the armed wing of the Marxist PKK had been fighting street by street against their militarily stronger opponent. If PKK won ISIS would lose the supply and escape route linking it with Syria, Mosul and Erbil. If ISIS won, there was a likelihood of another massacre of Yazidis and the Islamists would gain control over much of the Kurdish area of Iraq. The battle for Sinjar was thus a decisive one in the war against ISIS.

We had left the Peshmerga checkpoints far behind. Endless barley fields, stretching as far as the eye could see, slid past the car windows hour after hour. I was getting drowsy. In my dozy state I recalled the scenes of my first visit to the region. At that time, I had thought it was only a matter of time until ISIS beat the Kurds and conquered Mount Sinjar.

Like many others I had been mistaken. Now, five months on, we were on the winding roads leading up Mount Sinjar. In fields and on hillsides could be seen white tents with international charity logos on them. Thousands of refugees were still living on the mountain, afraid to return to their villages in case

ISIS struck again. When we reached the top of the mountain we stopped, had a smoke and waited for the PKK commander's permission to proceed. Down below us was Sinjar city, the old Yazidi stronghold.

Before ISIS overran the area the city's population was nearly forty thousand. By now most of the inhabitants had fled if they hadn't been killed or taken as slaves, and Sinjar was a ghost town. PKK controlled about three tenths of the municipal area, ISIS the rest. Now from the mountain top we saw a toy city spread out below in the spring sunshine. At frequent intervals a spurt of smoke would shoot up in the surrounding hills and, seconds later, the boom of an explosion would echo all round. We got back in our car and drove down into the town. None of us spoke as we stared at wrecked cars and ragged bits of clothing by the roadside, pathetic remnants, silent reminders of horror, evidence of the terrified exodus of townsfolk the previous August. As we approached the town centre the sickly smell of decomposing bodies filled our noses.

Among the ruins I unexpectedly came across Agir. Someone had told him a German reporter was in town, so he had set out and gone around all the posts manned by his comrades to find me and have a bit of German speaking practice. I was sitting in an armoured Humvee heading for the front line when suddenly a young man came up to the window, looked inside with a friendly smile and asked me in German where I was from. Shots were being fired outside, shells were exploding, but that didn't bother Agir who wanted a chat. "Come along, I bake cake for you," he said, offering me a cigarette. "Not a good idea, son, having conversations in the middle of the street," complained the driver, patting Agir on the arm and moving on. Agir waved and called after us, "Cake, yes? I wait!"

So, cake it was.

The next few days Agir hardly left my side. He was a 25-year old Kurd, a giant with the grip of a boxer and the disposition of a hamster. Everything about him seemed a bit larger than life: his impressive six-pack, his huge nose, his bulging biceps, his luxuriant moustache. He had a green and black cloth wound around his head, and he smoked.

A USAF jet roared over the gun placement where Agir was posted and dropped a bomb which exploded much too near for comfort. The ground quaked, the blast made the walls rattle and shook dust from the ceiling. A cloud of dust and smoke rose outside. Agir and his mate Adnan both flung themselves on the floor. I spilt my tea on my trousers in fright and staggered to join them, holding my hands over my head as protection. Adnan cursed. "Don't worry," Agir said to me, putting a hand on my shoulder, "The Americans can't aim properly, but they're aiming at ISIS, not us!"

It was ten in the morning, that day the allies nearly killed their own side. Up till then it had been a peaceful morning. We'd been drinking tea and I'd been watching Agir as he lost his third chess match in a row with Adnan. We were in a building much damaged by artillery. The two young men were giggling like schoolboys. Agir slapped his thigh with his huge hand as Adnan took his queen. Just twenty metres away, the other side of a row of houses, was an ISIS gun placement.

A young female PKK fighter, coughing and covered in dust, her bright red hair braided in a thick plait, ran into the room and laughed to see the three of us cowering on the floor. "Get out of here quick," she advised, waving the radio she was holding. "The plane's coming straight back!"

We crept out of our hiding place. "Come, boy. We hide," growled Agir. We made our hurried way through the ruins, clambering through holes from one house to the next. Agir pointed to a building some eighty metres away, the other side of an open space. "Run fast, ISIS snipers get us," said Agir, counting to three. We sprinted across. Agir barged the iron door open with his shoulder, we stumbled up a spiral staircase and hid behind a wall.

Communication is a problem for the PKK, said Agir, panting for breath. Because the PKK had carried out many covert attacks on military and civilian targets in Turkey over the years the authorities in Europe and the USA considered it to be a terrorist organization and declined to supply its fighters with weapons. For the same reason the coalition would only communicate with the Kurdish Peshmerga, who were active in the hills around the town, and not with the PKK who were on the front line. Thus any warning about coalition air raids only reached the PKK indirectly and too late. "They think we terrorist, they no talk to us," said Agir. He scratched his head and tried to explain. The PKK passed information about ISIS movements in the town to the Peshmerga and the Peshmerga passed it on to the Americans. The Americans then told the Peshmerga when and where an air raid would take place. As in the childhood game of Chinese whispers important details often got lost in transit. "Marvellous idiotic, no?" asked Agir.

Agir and I squatted behind a wall waiting for the second bomb to drop and hoping we were far enough from danger. The fighter plane was still circling in the sky like a raptor seeking prey. We would hear it come nearer and block our ears, then it would turn away again. Some Kurdish soldiers were taking cover against a wall not far from us. While we waited Agir, pensively tweaking his flamboyant moustache with forefinger and thumb, told me about his former life in Germany.

In 1998 he had arrived with his parents and siblings in a small town in Baden Wurttemberg. His parents were poor Kurdish peasants who had sought asylum in Germany. Speaking softly with head bowed

Agir told me of the difficulty he had had in mastering the German language. He didn't like thinking about that time; his fellow pupils had teased and bullied him and they used to call him a "dirty Kurd" or a "shitty Turk". For them he was a foreigner who had no business there.

At some point Agir realized he would never be welcome. When at last he was able to form a few sentences in German he started to defend himself. Exchanges of swearwords and fisticuffs in the playground followed; the teachers always sided with the local boys. When he was a bit older Agir also got in trouble with the police. His parents told him he should try harder to fit in, since Germany was now his country, but secretly he never felt he belonged. He dropped out of school and wandered all over Germany, from Stuttgart to Munich and Munich to Hanover, working at Siemens, in car repair shops, in bakeries, anywhere where unskilled labour was wanted for a while. He opened a kebab shop in partnership with an uncle. But nothing came to anything. The insults of his schooldays pursued him into young adulthood. In the end he packed his bag and, without telling his parents, left the country which did not wish to have him.

Agir folded his huge hand into a fist and beat his chest over the heart. "I feel pain here. All the time." His memories still hurt, but was he angry too? No, not any more, it was pointless. Back in Turkey he joined the PKK. He hadn't spoken with his family members since then, eight years ago. Lost in thought, he fondled his rifle as he sat there on the stairs in the ruined house where we were taking cover. The wounded boy had metamorphosed: from Agir the shitty Turk he had become Agir the guerrilla fighter, and the PKK had become his family.

So now it was warfare instead of kebabs. He pointed to a yellow and red painted bicycle lying near the staircase and said he wanted to see children playing in Sinjar's streets once more. He was mentally leafing through the pages of his wartime memories and they gave him pain, specially the scenes after the offensive to dislodge the ISIS forces which had been sitting on Sinjar. That was four years ago. The Peshmerga, Yazidis, PKK and Syrian Kurdish army made a combined assault with air support from the international coalition. Taken by surprise the ISIS troops retreated, and then the full extent of their murderous activities and barbarism in Sinjar came to light. There were piles of corpses in the streets, mass graves, decomposing bodies, landmines planted in houses. For the first week or two the fighters did nothing but collect corpses, Agir said, and they could easily find them by following the smell of rotten flesh. Many of the dead were women, children and elderly men. Agir fell silent and pursued these grim memories in the privacy of his mind. Ash from his forgotten cigarette fell onto his trouser leg.

Agir glanced at the bicycle, shook his head as if he was trying to shake off a bothersome fly, then continued kneading his hands in silence for several minutes. A loud hissing sound as if the air was being ripped apart wrenched him from his reverie, and it was followed by an ear-shattering thud. The USAF bomber was attacking the ISIS position and its bomb had exploded less than a hundred metres in front of us. A grey column of smoke rose into the sky, pieces of masonry pattered down on the roof of our hiding place, PKK fighters yelled with joy. Agir stood at the window, his hands clenched, and smiled as he watched the smoke column gradually dispersing in the wind.

Keeping to the cover of walls we raced back towards Agir's camp. The ISIS fighters, roused by the air raid, were shooting at the PKK, bullets whizzed over our heads. "Faster!" yelled Agir. My heart was beating wildly, my bulletproof waistcoat was grating my back, sweat was dripping into my eyes. All I could think of was the next bit of wall, the next building; the outside world ceased to exist. A few more metres, then at last we squeezed through a hole in a wall and reached safety.

The air in Agir's camp was blue. The US bomb had missed its target again. Adnan, Agir's chess opponent, punched the sofa furiously. "The Americans have been trying to destroy that base for three days. And for three days they have been missing it. It's not good enough." He took an apple in his left hand and an orange in his right. "This is where *Da'ish* are," he said, indicating the apple. Then he imitated the drone of a plane and squashed the orange. "And that is where nobody is!" Meanwhile Agir was washing the dust from his face. An announcement was made on the radio: one Peshmerga had been shot by an ISIS sniper. "He peep over wall to watch air raid, he got bullet in his head," said Agir, pointing to his forehead. Adnan, who was still seething, lit a cigarette and took a deep puff, then tilted his head back and with his eyes closed blew smoke at the ceiling. "You calm down, brother," said Agir. Then he got up to go, saying he had some baking to do. "I bake the best cake in Kurdistan. You must try some. See you later!" and he hugged me goodbye.

In the ruins of Sinjar's old quarter, five hundred metres as the crow flies from Agir's camp, Jacko was lying on a mattress next to a hole in the wall, squinting down the telescopic sights of his sniper rifle. A wiry 35-year old with a high, creaking voice, he was the commanding officer of the PKK in Sinjar. In front of him, about fifty metres away, was the building in which the ISIS had their camp and which the air raid that morning had failed to hit. It was a two storeyed house with an arch in the centre. Its facade was peppered with bullet holes.

For what felt like an eternity Jacko lay there without moving, his finger on the trigger. Suddenly a head rose from behind a wall, a figure appeared in his sights, Jacko squeezed the trigger, the head disappeared. "Don't know whether I got him or not. Quite likely I did," said Jacko, reloading. Not long afterwards, listening in on the ISIS frequency, his comrades heard an ISIS fighter asking urgently for a doctor. Jacko sighed and said he didn't enjoy killing people but it was necessary. "I've seen the kind of things *Da'ish* do, and we can't let them get away with it." After a three-hour stint Jacko was relieved by a young fighter and went back to his quarters, a battered ruin with tiles and sacks in the windows instead of glass. Bloodstains and some graffiti in Arabic were a reminder that ISIS had once occupied the house. "*Allahu akbar*" was painted neatly on the wall.

It was late night and darkness covered Sinjar like a black sheet. The moon was casting silver light on the ruins and the silence was broken by snipers firing. The rattle of a machine gun came from a nearby building. "*Da'ish*," said Jacko, shrugging indifferently. Then a shell exploded; the dialogue of weapons never stopped. Jacko pointed to a mattress in the next room, indicating that I was to sleep there. It was too dangerous to walk through the streets as the ISIS snipers had image intensifiers and thermal imaging devices and so could detect any person moving around up to a kilometre away, even at night.

I thought of Agir's cake. Then I thought of the Peshmerga fighter who had been killed by ISIS. The prospect of spending the night a few metres away from the nearest ISIS position was hardly enticing.

Still, it was better than walking through the streets of Sinjar in the dark. As if Jacko had read my thoughts he patted me on the back and told me not to be afraid. "You're safe up here, we have guards in every building." He added that although the *Da'ish* were better equipped the PKK were the better fighters. I wasn't sure whether to be reassured or alarmed by this statement, but thanked him for his hospitality.

Apart from Jacko there were fifteen other men in the room, which served as operations control centre, arsenal, common room and dormitory. They came from Turkey, Iran, Iraq and Syria and none of them were over 25. For them Jacko was father figure, boss, exemplar, confidant and friend. Sixteen years ago Jacko had joined the PKK to fight the Turks after Turkish soldiers had killed his grandfather. In the flickering light of a kerosene lantern we sat cross-legged on the floor. I was the first foreign journalist to spend a night at the camp and a long question and answer session ensued. Facing me were well informed young men with a genuine desire to learn. Did I think of them as terrorists? Why did the German government help the Peshmerga with weapons but not them, the PKK, who were on the front line? ("Give us a few Milan rockets and armoured vehicles and we'll liberate Sinjar in days," Jacko put in, laughing hoarsely.) Did I have any religion? The men had heard about the emerging ultra-right parties and asked why xenophobia still existed in Germany. Why did the German government allow German citizens to join ISIS? Why didn't the coalition mount more air raids? Why, why why.

The men smiled kindly and asked their questions politely, though sometimes I felt as if I was facing an inquisition. I was relieved when a young man entered the room bearing a tray of roast chicken, tomatoes and potatoes. Supper! Together we dipped flatbread into the communal pan. Afterwards sweet tea was served, then some of the men sat on the couch to read Nietzsche and the works of Abdullah Öcalan, the PKK leader incarcerated in Turkey. Many of them could identify with Nietzsche as the philosopher was said to have got the idea for his book *Thus Spoke Zarathustra* from Yazidi people who venerated Zarathustra as a god. I sat next to Jacko, smoking and playing backgammon with him. One fighter played the Italian partisan song *Bella Ciao* on his smartphone and everyone joined in the refrain, "O bella ciao! Bella ciao! Bella ciao, ciao, ciao!" Then they all laughed and embraced each other.

The men addressed each other as "heval", meaning friend and brother. The atmosphere inside the ruined building was relaxed and for a moment I forgot the war and felt I was at some kind of youth gathering, I was ready to clap and sing along. Only when the hammering sound of machine gun fire came from the roof was I yanked back into reality. This was no youth camp. Life in the old quarter of Sinjar city was full of austerity. It had no electricity, no water to wash in, no phone lines and no internet. In many parts of the town the Marxists and the Islamists were just yards away from each other. The passage of time was measured by the snipers' shots.

Jacko's men had been hanging out there for four months. They were well trained and disciplined but had only Kalashnikovs and bazookas to counter the tanks and rockets of ISIS. They had enough weaponry to defend themselves but not enough to attack. Jacko reckoned his three hundred PKK fighters were facing about four hundred ISIS troops, though exact numbers were unknown. There were many foreigners on the ISIS side: languages overheard on their frequency band included Turkish, Turkmeni, various dialects of Arabic, Dari and English. Jacko's folk had once even eaves-dropped on a conversation in German.

Next morning, I was awoken by an explosion. A shell had landed in the street next to Jacko's camp. A young man came panting in. "Grab your weapons and come quick!" he cried and ran out again. Jacko's men hurried after him. Not wishing to remain alone I followed them. We dodged through ruined streets, passed barricades and makeshift screens made with sheets and blankets, crept from one building to the next, till at last the fighters took cover behind a wall in the inner courtyard of a house. There I met Adnan. Everything was under control, he told me reassuringly, ISIS had merely tried to take a PKK post. While Adnan was screwing a shell into his bazooka something exploded close by and pieces of shrapnel smattered the wall we were sheltering behind. Adnan closed his eyes, mouthed a silent prayer, stood up and aimed at the ISIS position, squeezed the trigger and ... nothing. He ducked down again, impatiently checked the firing mechanism, reloaded the shell, took aim once more, and still nothing happened. "Hurry up, Adnan!" someone called. Adnan sniggered and spread his arms to show there was nothing he could do. A comrade handed him another bazooka. I watched the pantomime and pictured the ISIS training their mortar gun on us. I got closer to the protecting wall as Adnan made his third attempt. This time it worked and there was a tremendous boom. Smoke swirled and Adnan was sent flying by the recoil. He quickly picked himself up and peeped cautiously over the wall to see whether his shell had hit home. Then he turned around with a grin and held his thumb up.

Instead of stopping for a few hours I stayed five days with Jacko. Each day he led me through parts of the town held by his fighters, who were both men and women. We passed ancient mansions and ruined battlements clinging to the mountainside. In places the opposing forces were so close to each other one only dared look across the road with a mirror. I talked to some women snipers who told me the ISIS soldiers were terrified of being shot by a woman, as then they would not go to paradise. We played chess and backgammon, drank tea, visited the trenches and took shelter in bunkers and behind sandbags.

War had taken hold of Sinjar. "Without heavy weapons and reinforcements we won't make any progress," Jacko told me. He was still hoping to get support from the West, things like weapons, rockets, night vision equipment, armoured vehicles. The battle for Sinjar offered the PKK a chance to get rid of their reputation as a Marxist terrorist group and become accepted by the Western powers as partners. The previous August a couple of dozen PKK fighters had saved the Yazidis from certain death after the Iraqi government troops had fled from the advancing ISIS force under the black flag of the caliphate. In April Cemil Bayik, the PKK second in command, had used a TV interview to apologize for the violent demonstrations which Kurds had mounted in Germany in the eighties and nineties. At the same time PKK leader Abdullah Öcalan, from his prison cell, had conducted peace talks with the Turkish government. Since then certain Western politicians had come forward to suggest it was time to take a fresh look at the PKK and in particular to support them in the fight against ISIS. "Yes, the battle against *Da'ish* is helping to improve our image," said Jacko, "but we need a lot more of these." He drew a thermal imaging telescope from its leather case and caressed it as tenderly as if it had been a beautiful girl.

Too many Kurds had perished already, said Jacko. He opened a drawer and pulled out a folder containing the names and photos of fallen PKK fighters. Fifty-seven earnest young faces. He leafed through the pages, tracing the names and images with a forefinger and pausing over some of them as he muttered a few words in Kurdish as if communicating with the deceased. Then he put the folder away and stroked the stubble on his chin with his palm. He seemed about to say something but his voice failed. He coughed, took a sip of tea and then declared, with mixed pride and pathos, that they had died for Kurdistan and for humanity. I asked whether it made him sad. He stared at me as if he hadn't understood the question. "Is there any finer way to die than as a martyr for one's motherland?" No, he envied those young men whose portraits were now hanging in so many Kurdish living rooms, beside the Kurdish flag on school walls and on lamp posts in towns where they fluttered in the breeze.

The morning I was leaving I once again met Agir, the gentle German-speaking giant. He was leaning against an armoured Dingo, looking sulky. "That cake, I bake special for you," he said reproachfully. Then a broad grin lit up his face and he embraced me. "Never mind, my boys eat plenty!" I asked him where he'd got the Dingo from. "Oh, long story, that!" It had been a gift from the German government to the Peshmerga, who had soon lost it to ISIS. Then the PKK had wrested it from them. "Now I drive!" he said, proudly showing off the bullet holes in the armoured windscreen and bonnet. Agir walked with me to the vehicle which was going to take me out of town and then took his leave. "Come back soon, friend!" he said. "You taste my cake!"

Sinjar sank behind. Thick black smoke was rising into the blue morning sky. Passing a field of rape studded with poppy flowers I was hit again by the smell of corpses from a mass grave.

I often thought of Sinjar and Agir in the weeks following my return home. I wanted to get back to them as soon as possible. And in May 2015 I indeed saw Agir again.

At first I just glimpsed a head pop down among the ruins. Zagros, Goran, Shwan, Kamal and Agir, five young men with youth still glowing in their faces, had been lying all morning in the baking sun, hidden behind a wall and waiting for a movement in the trench some eighty metres in front of them. Zagros, a gangling youth, had now seen his target. He left cover, stood there with legs apart and the bazooka on his shoulder, pulled the trigger. Once the shell had landed, presumably killing the ISIS fighters in the trench, and the smoke had cleared the PKK men started thumping each other in joy, doing high fives, hugging one another.

Agir lighted a cigarette which then did the rounds of the group. Each fighter took a long puff and inhaled deeply till ash fell from the smouldering tip. "Well done," said Agir in his deep voice, speaking to

Zagros the marksman. "Come on, lads, we'd better get out of here."

After their successful attack that morning the Kurdish guerrilla fighters abandoned their post, as they knew ISIS would quickly target it with their mortars. Doubled up, they ran over a street where enemy snipers were waiting and made their way amid the ruins, creeping through holes in the walls from building to building. The houses here were simple two storeyed ones. The men walked through rooms where Yazidi families had once had their tea, sung their children to sleep, eaten supper together, watched Turkish films. Time had stopped. The ruins were mute witnesses to the horror meted out on the inhabitants by ISIS when they took over Sinjar the previous August, massacred the men, took the women and girls as sex slaves or unwilling brides for their fighters. Little things spoke of the terror of those who managed to flee: plates with the dry remains of an unfinished meal; a suitcase on the floor, hurriedly packed but never carried away.

In one deserted living room Agir bumped his great shoulder against a bookcase which fell over with a crash, sending up clouds of dust. Stooping to lift it he spotted a photograph album among the debris. He picked up the album and turned the pages, revealing memories of someone's happy days: children playing; a wedding; a smiling couple, the man in a suit and the woman in a dress; a picnic by a reservoir; outings to Baghdad, Erbil and the Yazidis' holy town of Lalish.

In this war the Marxists of the PKK and its Syrian equivalent the YPG had proved the most effective agents against the cruel hordes of the Islamic State: they had successfully liberated Hassaka, Tel Abyad, Kobane and Ras al-Ain from ISIS occupation, and now Sinjar was to follow.

But since Kurdish activists had attacked police stations in Turkey and Turkish planes had bombed PKK bases in Iraq the situation had got more complicated. In the name of defeating ISIS Turkey's president Erdogan had declared war on the Islamic State's greatest enemy. Concerned lest the Kurds, emboldened by their military success against ISIS, might declare an independent state of their own the Turkish government had thus opened another front in the war. Reliable news gets lost in conflict: the Turkish military claimed that nearly four hundred PKK fighters had been killed in air raids while the then commander in chief of the PKK, Murat Karayilan, maintained that a mere thirty "martyrs" had been plucked from his ranks, whereas 250 Turkish soldiers had been killed. Meanwhile in the Kurdish part of Turkey virtual civil war prevailed: street battles were taking place between Kurdish youths and Turkish soldiers and there was a daily death toll on either side. The PKK were still fighting ISIS in northern Iraq, but were they to withdraw and go to confront their old enemy Turkey ISIS would be free to unleash new terror in the region.

At the end of May there was still no sign of
Turkey drawing a line under the past. I arrived in
Sinjar in the back of an armoured vehicle late one
Sunday afternoon. Thick black smoke was rising over
the ruins. Agir was waiting for me. He grabbed me
and planted a juicy kiss on each of my cheeks.
"How's things? You OK? What you doing here?" he
asked in German, with a huge smile under his
awesome moustache. "Cake, Agir. You offered me
cake. That's why I'm here!"

Each day Agir took me to parts of the city held by
PKK. We drank tea in stately piles hundreds of years
old, chatted with fighters in battered ruins, played
chess and backgammon behind barricades of
sandbags. Moments of normality belied the general
chaos. I met some girl snipers who would squint for
hours down their telescopic sights till they saw an
ISIS man in the crossed hairs. After firing the bullet,
they would taunt the enemy, saying the dead man
would not go to paradise as he had been shot by a
woman. Then they would titter like little girls, cut a
notch in the butt of their rifles and put a fresh bullet
in the firing chamber. I met young Yazidis who had
joined the PKK to take revenge after ISIS had
burned their villages, killed their friends and relations,
abducted their sisters or daughters. "ISIS is a bane of
the 21st century which must be got over. It threatens
not only the Kurds, not only the Shiites, but all
humanity. It represents a perverse ideology which has
nothing to do with Islam," one sharpshooter told me

in one of the trenches. People everywhere kept asking me the same questions: Why doesn't the West support the PKK against *Da'ish*? Why don't you carry out more air raids? Do you really think the PKK is a terrorist group? They asked these questions without any hostility; they felt merely offended and disappointed. However often these questions were posed to me I had no answers beyond empty phrases.

Coalition fighter planes had been flying sortie after sortie all day long and one of the shells had hit a nearby house. We were sitting in the ruined building into which Agir's unit had moved; blankets and pieces of cloth had been drawn over the windows to stop light shining out. Agir shared the room with ten other fighters, who were now dozing on their decayed mattresses. Some lay reading the works of the PKK leader Abdullah Öcalan by torchlight, some were smoking in silence, some played backgammon while some just stared into space. Mosquitoes clustered around them to suck their blood, flies buzzed at their faces. In a building the other side of a courtyard were the Kurdish women fighters, the ones the ISIS fighters dreaded because if they were killed by a woman they might not go to paradise or get their seventy-two houris. "Them are crazy," said Agir, tapping his forehead with his finger. Then he explained the equal rights policy of the PKK. The only thing that was not allowed was flirtation. The men vowed to remain celibate like monks in a monastery, as directed by their leader Öcalan. "We have only one lover, Kurdistan," said Agir in a voice full of emotion. I was baffled: no mixing, no affairs, no sex? Not even any secret cuddling when no-one was looking? "Come on, Agir, tell me the truth," I said, needling him. "I know you've got some pretty girls somewhere," He gave me a dirty look.

Agir had no desire to talk about love and girls; he wanted to play. From his breast pocket he produced a folded laminated board and two dice: snakes and ladders, a game I'd often played with his mate Adnan on my first visit. I asked him how Adnan was. "He dead," Agir replied, smiling and gently smoothing the board with his fingers. "He give his life for Kurdistan one week ago." He told me how one night his friend had come to his bedside, handed the snakes and ladders over to him and said farewell, he was going to die. He had taken his rifle, strapped a belt full of hand grenades around his waist and strode out. He had then walked right inside the ISIS lines to kill as many of the enemy as possible. His body had been strung up, and it stayed dangling from a lamp post for days. Could there be a more beautiful death than that, Agir asked, and it sounded as if he was envious of his friend. Adnan the sharpshooter was the fifty-ninth PKK soldier to die in Sinjar. He was a quiet fellow, just 22 years old, who used to wear a funny hat and wanted to quit smoking.

A young woman stuck her head through the doorway and said nobody should leave the room as an air raid was about to begin. We switched our torches off and lay flat on our mattresses. I asked Agir how far away the *Da'ish* were. "Fifty metre," he replied. Nothing could be seen in the room except the glowing tips of cigarettes, dancing like fireflies in the darkness. All was quiet. Then we heard the plane coming; its distant hum rapidly growing louder. It circled overhead for a minute or two, then there was a loud whistling sound as if something was slicing the air, then a deafening boom. The explosion made the walls shake, debris rattled down on the roof, a cloud of dust came through the windows. Everyone started coughing against a smell of cordite and melted plastic. My eyes were smarting and I pulled a blanket over my head. A second bomb followed, then a third and a fourth. They fell so near, the blast reached us before we heard the explosion. Agir tickled my arm. "No worry," he said, "I keep my eye on you."

The morning after the bombardment thick black smoke hung over Sinjar like a storm cloud. The sound of machine gun fire echoed from the mountain slopes. Agir looked at the sky and pulled at his moustache. He said *Da'ish* were burning rubbish and car tyres so the pilots wouldn't be able to see what was going on in the town. They were quite likely to launch an attack in revenge for the air raid. The PKK fighters started taking up their positions ready to defend the town. But Agir wasn't among them; today he was on kitchen duty. He sat cross-legged on the floor, humming as he cut chicken into pieces, peeled potatoes, sliced tomatoes and boiled rice. Just when he was going to put the baking tray in the oven ISIS attacked his base. He looked at the food in annoyance, shook his head, grabbed his rifle and ran out. Bullets whizzed through the air, shells exploded. Agir stood behind a pile of sandbags, a stub of cigarette in his mouth, firing at an invisible opponent on the other side of the street. Forty minutes later the battle was over and Agir stumped back into the kitchen to finish cooking the meal.

Two days later I left Sinjar. We drove up the winding road leading from the town up to the top of Mount Sinjar. Looking out of the window I saw burned-out wrecks of cars. By the side of the road lay pieces of clothing belonging to slaughtered Yazidis. Beside me was a mournful Yazidi fighter on leave from the front, going to visit his betrothed in one of the many displaced peoples' camps, those bleak settlements of tents where hundreds of thousands of people were living as refugees in their own country. At the top of the mountain we stopped, had a cigarette and looked down into the valley. Below us Sinjar was shimmering in the sun like an assemblage of toy houses. I wondered how one could counter an opponent who beheaded journalists, sold women in slave markets like cattle, sanctioned the rape of nine-year-old girls, kept prisoners in cages to be burned alive or drowned in a river and demolished ancient temples which belonged to the cultural heritage of humanity. A plane flew over us and dropped a bomb.

On the horizon a black mushroom of smoke rose into the sky over Sinjar.

In November 2015 I was sitting in a restaurant in the city of Dohuk when I received the phone call I was waiting for. My long term fixer and friend Hassan told me to "get ready immediately." I was going to witness the liberation of Sinjar he said and told me to wait at a certain junction at the outskirts of the city. After months of debating and discussions, setbacks and arguments, the Kurdish factions and its allies finally agreed on the terms of who, how and when Sinjar was going to get liberated. Hassan mentioned that someone was going to pick me up at the meeting point he described. Soon after I was standing on a busy road, hoping to hitch a ride to Sinjar. After a while, a white van stopped and I squeezed in with fifteen armed men and one general. Because of my long time reporting on the Yazidis I had gained the trust of some Kurdish generals and PKK cadres. They smuggled me through the Peshmerga checkpoints. At the dawn of battle for the liberation of Sinjar the area became off limits to foreign journalists. I was lucky. We arrived late at night, and the general dropped me off the PKK headquarters at the foot of Mount Sinjar. Coalition aircraft had been bombarding IS positions nonstop for days. Kurdish Peshmerga fired their artillery into the city from the top of the mountain.

The next morning Kurdish units moved in from the West and East, ten thousand armed men with tanks, supported by air strikes, got a firm grip on Sinjar, captured Highway 47, the connecting road between Raqqa in Syria and Mosul in Iraq, which were the strongholds of the Islamic State, and thus cut-off one of the most important supply lines of the extremists. I waited with PKK troops in the in the old town of Sinjar.

For 15 months I had been reporting on the situation in Sinjar and the suffering of the Yazidis. I was excited that the wait was finally over. I was the only foreign journalist in the city. This was a historic day for the Yazidis, and I had the privilege to witness this. Kassim Khalaf, a 22-year-old Yazidi stood on top of a small hill among some two hundred fighters, eager and impatiently awaiting the signal to attack ISIS positions below. That morning, his commander intercepted a radio call, in which an ISIS emir ordered his fighters to burn all the documents and abandon the city. "The cowards are fleeing," Kassim murmured, visibly disappointed. After ISIS overran the region in August 2014, kidnapped, enslaved and murdered thousands of Yazidis, Kassim, like so many others, took to arms and joined the Kurdish Workers' party. Since then he was constantly fighting.

A cold wind blew down from the mountain slopes this morning. Kassim closed the zipper of his leather jacket and jumped from one foot to the other to keep himself warm. Shortly before 10 a.m. the PKK commander finally gave the signal the male and female Kurdish and Yazidi fighters were waiting for 15 long months: attack! Kassim and the other fighters stormed down the hill screaming from the top of their lungs, penetrated ISIS controlled quarters, ran from streets to street, until they reached the and end of the city - without firing a single shot, encountering hardly any resistance from the last remaining ISIS cells. They had fled without a fight. The fighters looked at each other puzzled. After that they broke out in cheers, hugged each other. Many had tears in their eyes. Yet, a few ISIS fighters had been hiding in the rubble, they were killed immediately. Their dead bodies were lying in the under the sun.

It was Friday, the 13th of November 2015, 10:30 am. Sinjar was finally liberated, instead of the black banner of the Islamic State, the flags of the many Kurdish militia are now blowing above the ruins. It took fifteen dreadful months to chase ISIS out of Sinjar. And just a few weeks ago it did not look like the extremists would give up without a fight. Sinjar was liberated, but also reduced to rubble. Kassim Khalaf, the young Yazidi fighter was a bit disappointed that there was hardly any resistance and that he could not kill anyone for satisfy his thirst for revenge. He was standing next to the body of an IS fighter, who was killed in an air raid the day before and fired shots of joy into the air. "Hol Hola Tausî Melek'a!" he screamed in joy and tied the flag of the Yazidi People's Defense units onto a lamppost.

A car drove by and stopped because cheering crowds were blocking the street. A captured IS fighter sat in the back of the pick-up truck, next to the body of a fallen PKK fighter. His hands were tied behind his back and he was shaking with fear, terror is his eyes, convinced that he was going to be soon executed. A young, angry Kurd starting hitting the man in the face, spat at him and yelled that he was going to kill the prisoner to revenge his family which were killed by ISIS. A PKK soldier interfered, calmed the man down and said that Kurds don't kill prisoners.

Meanwhile, I saw some Peshmerga soldiers looting shops and houses, they loaded fridges, mattresses and TVs on trucks. A couple of soldiers poured gasoline over the body of an ISIS fighter and set him on fire. The PKK, who watched this, shook their heads in disgust and spat in the dust. "This is a behavior we cannot tolerate", one female fighter told me. "This is not how we treat our enemies." In the chaos and joy of the liberation, I had lost young Kassim Khalaf, whose job it was to protect me. I filmed PKK fighters performing victory dances and triumphantly fired their rifles into the air. They chanted slogans and sang songs of victory. One of the fighters, whom I knew from previous visits, hugged me and kissed my cheeks. "Freedom. Finally!", he whispered in my ear, jumped onto a truck and stretched out his hand to me. I had no idea where they were going, but everyone was celebrating, dancing, laughing. It was a strange sensation, a peculiar sense of satisfaction. I was aware of the magnitude of this days. I had witnessed history.

But I was alone in a liberated city and my translator was nowhere to be found. So I climbed onto the truck as well. I was curious where it would take me. The truck sped through the streets until it reached the cement factory at the end of the town. Just hours before the black flag of the Islamic State was still blowing in the wind at the top of the silos. This factory was the highest and strategically most important building in Sinjar. When I arrived, PKK fighters were just in the process of hanging a huge banner of the Kurdish Workers Party on one of the silos; yellow and green with a red star. Shortly thereafter I got a glimpse into the future of Kurdistan: I became a witness to an internal quarrel between the victorious Kurdish factions. While the PKK was marking its territory, Kasim Shesho, the Yazidi General, commissioned by the Kurdish President Masud Barzani, triumphantly drove into the vestibule of the factory with about fifty of his own fighters. I was happy to see them and waved at a few well-known faces. I congratulated the general.

The adrenalin started to fade and I realized that I had not eaten or slept in over twenty-four hours. I was exhausted. I sat down and watched as Shesho's fighters hoisted a giant Kurdish flag - red, white and green with a bright sun in the middle - from one of their truck. It was easily fifty meters long and twenty meters high and could have probably covered the entire front of the factory. Shesho's fighters were commanding the PKK to take down their flag so they could honor the Kurdish victory with the flag of the Peshmerga. "This is our city, our victory," Sheshos men said. "Leave. You have no business here." The PKK commander kept calm said, that his fighters conquered the factory and therefore their insignia will remain. End of story. The Yazidis should find another building to hoist their flag. After all, the city was big enough for all of them. It was starting to get a little bit nasty, insults were thrown, voices raised, fists shaken in anger. General Shesho argued endlessly with the PKK leader while their fighters insulted and jostled each other. An American fighter jet flew over the factory. The pilot wobbled the wings a few times. A congratulatory greeting to the allies down below in the city. The men quarreling on the ground did not even notice the honor. They were too busy arguing and marking their territories.

I watched the scene, shaking my head in disbelief. ISIS was defeated, yet it took only a few hours to find new enemies amongst each other over ideological and political enmities. I was too tired to film the petty fight. But I was aware that this dispute between the victors was only a pre-taste of the tensions to come in the future. It was only a matter of time until an inner-Kurdish struggle for political interpretation and territorial claims would break out in the region.

After an hour or so of shouting, the PKK finally took their flag down, and soon afterwards the Peshmerga sun shone from the factory silos. Sheshos Yazidi fighters took pictures of each other, made victory signs and posed with their weapons. Once all pictures were taken they jumped back onto vehicles and raced off. I was so tired that I dozed off for a while.

When I woke up, I was all alone at the cement factory. The PKK had left as well and did not offer me a ride back to the city center. It was eerily quiet. I had no other choice but to walk back to the city. The streets were totally empty. To the left and right shot up ruins and bombed houses. I walked towards downtown Sinjar and remembered that ISIS had mined the entire city. Worse still, the city had not been searched and cleared of IED's and mines. Some IS-fighters and sleeper cells could still be hiding in the ruins or in the secret tunnel system under the city. I realized: there was no one here to protect me. Hallelujah.

My phone had no signal, so I could not contact anyone to pick me up and get me out of this embarrassing situation. A car came from the direction into which ISIS had fled. Suicide bomber, I thought immediately. I could not hide in the ruins on either side of the road because they were possibly mined. I started to run, knowing perfectly well how ridiculous the idea was to run away from a car in full speed on a straight road. After a few meters I was out of breath. I was tired, I wore my flag jacket and carried my camera. The car pulled up next to me. A Peshmerga stuck his head out of the window, surprised to see a foreigner walking alone through Sinjar. "What are you doing here alone?" he asked. "It is very dangerous, you know. Da'ish could still be here." Thank you very much, I was very much aware of that, I thought. "Come on, jump in the car. I'll take you into town", the man said with a sympathetic smile. I did as I was told.

The Peshmerga was one of general Sheshos fighters. He told me that just minutes ago two of the general's vehicles carrying his men drove over a mine on the way back from the cement factory. Five Yazidi died, dozens were seriously wounded. The driver dropped me in the city where I bumped into Kassim, my protective detail who got lost in the victory celebrations. "Where have you been?", he asked and gave me a hug. One day after liberation, Kurdish units uncover three mass graves, including one with the remains of seventy elder women. It was the first of many mass graves to be found in the coming weeks and months.

　　While Sinjar was being liberated, ISIS members attacked Paris. Three suicide bombers detonated themselves outside the Stade de France in Saint-Denis, during a football friendly between France and Germany. Meanwhile, armed men shot at people outside the bar Le Carillon and killed people dining inside the restaurant Le Petit Cambodge. At the same time gunmen carried out a mass shooting and took hostages at an Eagles of Death Metal concert in the famous Bataclan theatre. 130 people were murdered this day, another 413 were injured.

Chapter 16: Rojava, February 2016

As 2016 began the Islamic State was still a dismal reality. However, it was being bombed from the air by a multi-national coalition all over Iraq and Syria. In Syria a new warring faction was emerging, one which had hoped to keep out of the civil war: the Kurds. They were pushing IS further and further back and had by now become the West's most reliable partner. In February 2016 I got the chance to travel to the Kurdish controlled zone in Syria.

The journey took me past the killing fields of the previous year. Amude, Ras al-Ain, Tel Abyad, a place which had been in IS hands until July. I passed grim relics of a reign of terror: iron cages in which the Sharia police incarcerated persistent smokers; village squares where victims' heads had been displayed on poles. I reached Kobane, the town which became a symbol of the fight against the IS, then left the Kurdish heartland and went on into the liberated Arab areas of Aleppo province, driving for hours along empty roads through unpopulated no man's lands. I saw abandoned villages with bombed houses whose inhabitants had fled months earlier to Turkish refugee camps or to Iraq, some even crossing the Mediterranean Sea to Europe. Altogether the journey from Erbil in northern Iraq to Barhot in Syria took fourteen hours. Barhot was where I would meet Abu Abdullah

Shortly before 10 o'clock on that February morning a man in a mask carrying a Kalashnikov approached Abu Abdullah's hiding place. "Seven Islamists have crept up to within four hundred metres," the masked man announced. Abu Abdullah glanced at his watch, stiffened and considered the situation. Normally the IS people fired a few Katyushka rockets at this post around this time. His location was Barhot, a small settlement on the very edge of Aleppo province, about fifty-five kilometres from Raqqa.

Abu Abdullah was in charge of a unit of hardened fighters calling themselves Ahrar al-Raqqa or the liberators of Raqqa. Nine men and one fifteen-year old boy, they had dug themselves in here, among the crumbling abandoned mud houses and desiccated wilderness of Barhot. Ahrar al-Raqqa were part of the Syrian Democratic Forces (SDF), a military alliance set up the previous October which included Kurdish, Sunni Arab, Assyrian Christian and Turkmeni units; altogether around forty thousand fighters, women as well as men, of which thirty thousand were Kurds. They had been transforming the war situation in Syria and were now considered the most reliable ground troops and the best partners of the West in its fight against IS. The four thousand Arabs among them had so far been little more than a symbolic presence, but with every village in the Syrian heartland which the SDF reconquered another section of the Free Syrian Army was joining them.

Among these were the Revolutionary Army, an amalgam of several FSA units.

Life in this place was extremely dangerous. Just last night a group of Islamists had tried to take over Abu Abdullah's position. His men had been able to repel the attack but ammunition was now running low. Abu Abdullah received a radio message telling him that a suicide bomber had blown himself up at Ain Issa, twenty kilometres away. Abu Abdullah gave orders to fire on any vehicle which approached the post without warning.

The commander left his bunker and, wrinkling his eyes against the winter sunshine, climbed the staircase to a turret where a lone rebel was peering into the vacant desert with his binoculars. Ahead was the last bastion defending the shrinking domain of the black caliph Abu Bakr al-Bagdadi. Only metres away a low narrow trench one-kilometre-long, more of a symbol than a barrier, marked the boundary of the caliphate. A US fighter plane was drawing a vapour trail in the sky and a Predator drone was humming above the IS post. An east wind was blowing as Abu Abdullah silently gazed in the direction of his native city Raqqa.

Abu Abdullah was a thin handsome 25-year old with a carefully trimmed beard and a soft voice. On his head he wore a yellow and brown *kufiya*, the traditional headdress of Arab men. His thick dark locks fell down to his shoulders.

The young commander sat on a dirty mattress in his private cubbyhole. The February chill was softened by heat from a stove. Abu Abdullah had a radio and a kalashnikov beside him. He looked at his hands, which he kept rubbing together as if to rid them of dirt, and began his tale.

It began in March 2013. As soon as the IS executioner shot the first of the eleven condemned men in the head, in the middle of Naim Square in Raqqa, Abu Abdullah knew this was not the Syria he belonged to. This was not what he wanted to fight for. Like most of the inhabitants of his quarter he stood in the crowd and watched the gruesome spectacle in horror. One dictatorship had replaced another, he thought. The masked executioner went up to the next man, who was kneeling in front of him, and fired. Afterwards the men in black dragged the bodies from the pool of blood and crucified them on iron frames. Those men were Alawi traitors, the IS killers had declared. Then and there Abu Abdullah had vowed to fight against the Islamic State.

Months before that ugly drama, in the autumn of 2012, Abu Abdullah had locked up his little tailoring shop in a Raqqa back street to join the revolution against President Bashar al-Assad.

Together with his four brothers Abu Abdullah had been fighting since then for justice in Syria. First the five young men joined the Liwa Thuwwar al-Raqqa, the revolutionary brigade for the liberation of Raqqa.

In March 2013, in alliance with the al-Qaida offshoot Jabhat al-Nusra and other Islamic groups plus units of the FSA, they had driven the last of the government troops out of the city. Raqqa had been liberated, the first place in Syria to throw off Assad's rule. But their joy did not last long; soon afterwards the IS declared Raqqa to be the capital of their caliphate. Disillusioned and cowed, Abu Abdullah and his brothers fled to a refugee camp in Turkey.

In October 2015 Abu Abdullah had returned home and joined the SDF. A deeply religious Sunni Muslim, he wanted to fight for a Syria in which every person could live in accordance with his or her beliefs. At that point in his narrative Abu Abdullah broke off, took his Quran and disappeared into the next room, as it was time for his midday prayers.

At a point when the war in Syria was getting particularly brutal and confused the multi-ethnic and multi-religious SDF offered fresh hope to moderate Syrians. With every victory won by the alliance the myth of the Islamic State's invincibility crumbled further. Under the leadership of the Kurdish YPG and with air support from the US-led coalition the alliance had managed in the past months to push IS back into its core area in Syria. Royava, West Kurdistan, had been liberated. In late February SDF forces had driven the last Islamists out of Shadadi in Hassakeh province in north-western Syria. In Aleppo province they advanced west as far as Manbij. At Ain Issa in Raqqa province Kurdish and Arab troops waited impatiently for the long planned assault on Raqqa itself.

Abu Abdullah's story took me back to 2012. The young man was speaking with the voice of the Syrian revolution in its earliest days, a voice full of hope for better times. How had he preserved that hope through years of darkness without being radicalized like so many others? I was intrigued. Maybe hope still existed for Syria in the shape of men like him, religious but not fanatic. He would be Syria's future, if he survived the war.

The main winners of the war so far seemed to be the Syrian Kurds. Since managing to hold Kobane, not without heavy losses, against a much stronger IS force they had gone on from one victory to another. In July 2014 the Syrian Kurds controlled only a narrow strip along the Turkish border whereas by the start of 2016 they with their allies had conquered an area three times as large as the Lebanon. Setting up the Syrian Democratic Forces had been a good tactical move and a smart bit of rebranding. For long the Kurdish YPG had been seen as an effective and reliable force in the fight against IS yet still something of a terrorist pariah thanks to its ideological association with Kurdish figurehead Abdullah Öcalan, head of its sister organization PKK, who had been jailed in Turkey. That was why virtually all the Kurdish rebel units had now rallied under the respectable flag of the SDF. However, the fact that the Syrian Kurds were gaining political respectability in the war vexed Turkey, a NATO member, which viewed them as an even greater security risk than the IS.

Especially now that they were on the point of making their most significant gain, which was to create a corridor linking the Kurdish enclave Afrin with Kobane and Jazira. Thus for the first time in their history the Kurds would be in control of a unified area stretching from the north western tip of Syria right across its northern edge bordering the Turkish frontier to the far eastern side of Iraq. In order to achieve this goal since the beginning of February SDF and YPG troops had been advancing from Afrin to Azaz, just five kilometres from the Turkish frontier. They had taken the air force base at Mennigh and the villages Kefir Naya and Kefir Neris; the towns of Tel Riffat and Marea were about to fall to them. The SDF claimed to be attacking only IS, al-Qaida and other Islamist groups, but some rebel militias supported by the USA and Turkey, which had long been the main bulwark against IS and the Assad regime in northern Syria, fell foul of the Kurds if they got in their way. So it came about that different US-sponsored elements of the rebellion were fighting each other. It was as if the Pentagon was at war with the CIA. The only party to benefit from this was Assad; the Turks were exasperated, though on the other hand the Russians were glad.

The fraught political background hardly bothered Abu Abdullah and his men. "We joined the SDF because only if we unite can we defeat *Da'ish*," said Abu Abdullah, lighting a new cigarette from the stub of the previous one and inhaling deeply. Wisps of smoke escaped from his mouth as he added, "*Da'ish* first, then the Assad regime." At the moment all that mattered was the immediate goal, Raqqa. The war had claimed four cousins of his and his eldest brother, Mohammed, was lying in a Turkish hospital riddled with bullets. During lulls in the fighting he thought about his family members still living in Raqqa. He hadn't been able to speak to his mother for seven months. His wife's parents supported IS and had forbidden their daughter to join him. He thought of his elder son, four-year-old Abdullah, and of two-year-old Abdelkarim who had been born after he had quit Raqqa and whom he had never seen. "I pray daily for my family, that they may survive, and I think of them all the time," he said, closing his eyes.

The cold of night gave way to the heat of day as Abu Abdullah told his tale. Three hundred metres behind his post the yellow and green flag of the YPG fluttered over a farm building. Near it a unit of Kurdish women fighters was encamped.

Was this new military alliance just a stratagem of the Kurdish movement aimed at extending its influence amid the confusion of war while skilfully playing off Russian, Turkish and American interests against each other? An adviser of the Syrian government had recently announced that the SDF had made a pact with government troops, something the SDF command immediately denied. Could the alliance serve as the blueprint for a peaceful settlement in Syria after the fall of IS? Be that as it may, the leaders of the Syrian Kurds were playing a clever game with Russian and American interests and edging nearer to their goal: an independent Kurdish state.

In order to find out more I had to go back to Kobane. There, next to a yard piled with the wrecks of armoured vehicles damaged in the battle for the town, Ismet Sheikh Hassan was sitting in his office feeling annoyed because his tea had no sugar in it. As a result of a Turkish-Iraqi blockade no sugar had been available for days.

"We are getting no cement for reconstruction, no milk powder for the children, no drugs for patients," he complained. The 51-year old defence chief of Kobane district was a stocky but elegant man with grey hair and moustache. He was wearing a suit and an overcoat against the cold. Above him hung photos of Kurdish fighters, male and female, who had been killed in action and a larger than life size portrait of Kurdish leader Öcalan stared down from another wall. The previous day a suicide bomber had blown himself up in Ankara killing twenty-eight other people. Less than twelve hours after the event the Turkish authorities identified the assailant as a Syrian

Kurd, a member of YPG; but they were wrong, and subsequently the Freedom Falcons of Kurdistan (TAK), a radical offshoot of PKK, admitted responsibility for the attack.

"Collaboration with the Syrian regime is not an option," said the minister categorically, barring an incoming phone call as he sipped his tea. How could anyone cooperate with people who were responsible for so much death and suffering? The aim was to change the system and stop injustice in Syria as a whole, not just in Kurdistan. One bit of Syria couldn't exist without the others. "We've no problem with Russia as such, but as it's supporting the regime we will accept no help from it."

Ismet Sheikh Hassan's thoughts left the future and drifted back into the past, which sat on the present like a layer of dirt. Before the revolution he had been a Kurdish activist and he had been detained by the Syrian secret service no fewer than nine times. Each time he had spent weeks or months in one prison or another, he had been tortured and his family had been harassed. The first goal was to conquer IS; then they would free Syria from all extremists, anyone who stood in the way of democracy. So far they hadn't got any weapons, at least not in Kobane. But in early February Barack Obama had sent his special adviser Brett McGurk to see them, maybe hoping to get an oar in before Russia did. They had been promised help, both political and military.

Militarily, at least, things were going all right even without help. Two hours from Kobane by car, on the bank of the Euphrates, lay the town of Tishrin. It had been occupied for two and a half years, first by the al-Nusra front, then by IS. In early January SDF troops with coalition air support had crossed the Euphrates and taken the Tishrin Dam, the main power source for Aleppo province. Twenty-five engineers were now working to repair it and restore power. The next goal was Manbij, and after that Jarablous. This way a broad corridor might be opened from the south to connect the Kurdish areas with the Syrian provinces of Aleppo and Raqqa, simultaneously cutting the Islamic State's supply routes between its Syrian strongholds. However, IS had been offering fierce resistance among the ruins of Tishrin. A few hours earlier a suicide bomber had crashed through road blocks in a car in order to blow himself up on the dam.

We followed a zigzag course to the front, passing ruins full of land mines where a black IS flag bearing the Islamic declaration of faith still hung on a wall. When the car was in range of IS snipers the Kurdish driver stepped on the gas and shrank down behind his steering wheel. He drew up in front of a small fortress of sandbags and mud walls. Seven Kurdish fighters were squatting on the roof keeping a sharp eye on the enemy soldiers in a trench hardly three hundred metres away.

When a sniper's bullets started whistling past his head Sherwan knew more trouble lay ahead. The IS had already shelled his post with rockets and mortars that morning. He crept behind a wall and peered with his binoculars through a gap between sandbags.

Sherwan, a 25-year old Turk of slight build, was in command of a Kurdish unit made up of seven men and two women. Some of these were former PKK fighters who had joined their Kurdish brethren in Syria to help them in their battle against IS. But there was also a waiter from Anatolia who had been fighting at the front for seven months. For many PKK fighters, trained in guerrilla tactics and used to mountain warfare, this asymmetrical SDF battle for villages and dams was new territory, Sherwan explained. Instead of a YPG badge on their uniform sleeves they now had the SDF one, a yellow badge with an outline map of Syria and 'Syrian Democratic Forces' written in Kurdish, Arabic and Aramaic. True, the IS had inflicted several defeats on them but they were still strong and well equipped, and they regularly mounted well planned counter-attacks. An IS fighter broke cover and the men on the roof opened fire. Sherwan looked through his binoculars again, but there was nobody to be seen.

In Tishrin too Kurds and Arabs were fighting side by side against a common enemy, the Northern Sun battalion. Here were PKK, YPG and Kurdish women brigades, plus an American volunteer. And on a hilltop, wrapped in a ski jacket, sat a blonde 25-year old German from Aachen, looking like a castaway in a strange land. In his pocket he had a German-Kurmanji dictionary. He called himself Karkar Almania, German Worker: a suitable moniker to show where he was from and to celebrate a well-known national characteristic. But he preferred not to mention his real name.

He was looking down into the valley, staring at villages still controlled by IS and feeling irked at how boring war was. There was no face to face combat, no urban warfare; it was disappointing. The equipment also left much to be desired. "Our vehicle depot is a dump, and we have too many lousy weapons and not enough good ones," he said. He had been in the rearguard at the battle for Tishrin, marching a lot, keeping watch, getting no response when he shot into the darkness.

The IS fighters knew they were defenceless against the devastating firepower of US fighter jets. "It's the air support which achieves the most; without them we'd have no chance," declared Karkar Almania, running a hand through his dishevelled hair. He had been fighting with the Kurds for seven months. After his school leaving exam he'd done optional military service in Germany. A year ago he had read on the internet that the YPG were recruiting foreign volunteers. People from America, Holland, Britain, New Zealand, Australia, Sweden, Canada, Poland, Denmark and Spain were pouring into northern Syria, as well as a few Germans. He had put a comment on a Facebook recruiting page saying he was prepared to enlist. Not long after that the Lions of Rojova had smuggled him via Iraq into Syria. Since then he'd moved from front to front but never done any real fighting. He wanted to stay until the Kurds had linked up their territories, then return to Germany on leave.

At the moment leave seemed a distant prospect. The following afternoon the SDF tried to take over two strategically important hills to the north and south of Tishrin. American jets flew one sortie after another, flying low over the IS positions to bomb them before climbing away again. Black mushrooms of smoke rose into the evening sky above Tishrin while SDF units stormed the hills. The battle continued into the night. Next day it was reported that eighteen IS soldiers had been killed, many weapons had been seized, a bomb factory had been destroyed and both hills had been taken. Kurdish and Arab fighters embraced each other and rejoiced at this new victory over IS.

I left Tishrin wondering how things would develop in Syria. It was only a matter of time until the IS was beaten, but what after that? At the root of the war was the regime in Damascus: as long as Assad stayed in power peace was impossible. Even if he stepped down there was no certainty of the participants in the war achieving unity. Five years of conflict, an estimated 400,000 plus killed, cities destroyed, a generation who had known nothing but war. It would take decades for the country to be built up again and the trauma people had suffered would never disappear.

Chapter 17: Cihan's World

Two hours away from Tishrin, in March 2016, I met the young man who was the initial reason for my trip: a leftist from Saarbrücken who hoped world revolution would start in Syria. Cihan Kendal was twenty-six years of age and his real name was once Marc; to protect his family he declined to reveal his surname. Cihan Kendal was a *nom de guerre* meaning something like "world at the abyss" – it seemed appropriate enough for the area he was in. He had joined the YPG and they had given me permission to accompany him for five days. Kendal, a slight figure, was friendly enough, but his first question to any visitor was about their political stance; he wanted to know their ideological hue before discussing other things with them. He had been in charge of a small unit of Kurdish fighters in Ain Issa since the beginning of 2016. His was the last outpost in the war against IS.

Well cocooned in a winter jacket, Cihan Kendal leaned against a wall. The morning sun was reflected in his glasses. He was wearing a loosely tied green head cloth and he wanted to tell me how happy he was: no-one could have a pleasanter life than he. "What more could I want? I'm doing the thing I wanted to do and I'm perfectly free." Pensively he stroked his rifle. He knew he might meet his death here. "I've lost several friends in this war, more than just a couple," he said quietly, blinking in the sun and turning his head aside. Most recently he had lost his commanding officer, friend and mentor. With seventeen comrades he had fallen into an IS ambush on 30th December 2015. All of them had been killed. A picture of his dead friend hung in his unit's common room next to a portrait of Abdullah Öcalan and a Kurdish flag. On Kendal's left forearm were tattooed the words 'No Justice', and on the right one 'No Peace'. "Without justice there is no peace, and without peace there is no justice," he explained. That was his life principle which, he said, enabled him to remain human even in wartime.

Remaining human was an issue. He said he didn't know how many enemy fighters he had killed; he didn't keep a tally. One could get used to killing and accept it as part of war, just as one could get used to the rough Spartan life: nothing but beans and couscous every day, no electricity or running water. But he could remember the first time he had to kill. Some memories were hard to blot out. "A suicide bomber was threatening to blow himself up. He was just a lad, seventeen or eighteen years old. We would have taken him prisoner but he refused to surrender. So there was no other choice. Sadly, one can't argue points with the IS." I asked him if he had felt pity for the boy. No, he said, pity was a luxury one could not afford in wartime.

When he talked of revolution it sounded as if the war around him didn't exist, as if none of it was there, the fear and suffering, the dead and wounded, the

friends he had lost. He spoke about his own role as if
he was a bit player in the last act of a great drama at
the end of which the world would be put to rights.
That was why he was there: revolution, man! Quite
normal.

Nothing was normal in the parched wilderness of
the Syrian province of Raqqa. Blankets of mist
floated over the battlefield on which Kurds and
Islamists had been waging a bitter tactical war for
months. One side might gain a few metres, then lose
them again the following day. Cihan Kendal clapped
his hands together to revive his frozen fingers. Since
three in the morning he had been on sentry duty on
the roof of the former waterworks on the edge of
Ain Issa, scanning the surroundings for the enemy
who were lurking in deserted farm buildings all
around.

Exactly seventeen years ago that day the Turkish
secret service had arrested the Kurdish leader
Abdullah Öcalan, Apo to his followers, in Kenya. In
1999 a Turkish court had sentenced Öcalan to death
for high treason, formation of a terrorist organization,
possession of explosives, robbery and murder. In
2002, the death penalty having meanwhile been
abolished, the sentence was commuted to life
imprisonment. The Kurdish People's Defence
Brigades (YPG) marked the anniversary of Öcalan's
detention with hours of contemplation and
abstinence. That day they were going to study the
writings of Apo and critically analyse their own

progress, noting what was satisfactory, what needed improvement, who had transgressed and so on. They would neither eat nor drink the whole day long. The hardest part would be not smoking.

Cihan Kendal was one of about 120 Germans fighting alongside the Kurds. What made him stand out from the other foreign recruits was that he hadn't come to kill Islamists or take revenge, but to pursue his ideals and work for what he thought was a better world. He had joined the Kurdish cause before the Islamic State had come into existence. He could speak the Kurdish language Kurmanji fluently, had shed his German identity and adopted Kurdish culture. His comrades looked on him as one of their own. For him the struggle against IS was the beginning of a world revolution, a step on the way to the establishment of a perfect society. He was an idealist but insisted he was no dreamer. He was sure the Syrian desert was where he could get closest to realizing his leftist utopia which would entail equality of the sexes, formation of a self-governing civil society, abolition of the state with its hierarchies; that was why he had left Germany. "I'm fascinated by the Kurdish revolution. It offers the possibility of creating a real alternative to capitalism. I'm ready to sacrifice my life for it."

Thousands of Kurdish men and women had already given their lives in the struggle against IS. Three Germans had also died. 19-year old Ivana

Hoffman from Emmerich am Rhein was killed on 7th March 2015. 21-year old Kevin Joachim from Karlsruhe had been one of Marc's best friends; he fell at the battle of Tel Abyad in July 2015. A 55-year old former German army soldier lost his life while Kurdish troops were retaking the town of Shadadi in March 2016. Those who had fallen were honoured as martyrs; their portraits graced the walls of Kurdish living rooms, hung beside the Kurdish flag and pictures of other martyrs in schools, fluttered like bunting on lamp posts in Kurdish towns. Kendal said it was painful to see so many friends die around one, but death was part of war. He had no illusions about that, and was not worried by it. "I don't intend to die here; I'm sure I will survive." He sounded as if he expected an invisible shield to protect him.

All in all, Kendal seemed to derive his confidence from the certainty that he was doing the right thing with his life. I asked him whether he ever had doubts. Kendal shook his head and looked at me as if he didn't understand the question. "There is no right life in a wrong life," he said, quoting Theodor Adorno. As to whether having fought with the Kurds against IS might have awkward consequences in Germany, the question didn't bother him, for he had no intention of returning to Germany. That chapter of his life was closed, he said. In future he would go wherever the Party of Democratic Union (PYD) sent him. Kurdistan was now his home, Kurdish comrades his family.

Cihan Kendal didn't wish to reveal much about his past, claiming it was over and done with. The little he did say gave at least a glimpse of his previous existence. His father had met with a fatal accident when Marc was five years old and his mother had brought him and his younger brother up single handed. "I'm thankful to my mother for making me the person I am," he said. From an early age he took an interest in politics and world affairs; he mugged up socialist theory, he attended demonstrations. He sought answers to a question that had bothered him since childhood: what is justice? He had always wondered whether it was permissible to use force to counter injustice and oppression, and that led him in the direction of radical socialism.

He couldn't find answers in bourgeois Saarbrücken so after leaving school he moved to the cosmopolitan city of Hamburg, a hotbed of alternative ideas. He protested against data storage, had fights with Nazis and policemen, did a year of voluntary work in a pre-school, did a bit of studying and started a group with like-minded friends where they discussed socialist utopia. Yet still he felt something was missing. The freedom of German society was surrounded by emptiness; studying, theorizing, demonstrating did nothing to fill the void with content. Then a lawyer he knew put him in touch with some Kurdish resistance fighters and that changed everything. He finally found the answers to his questions in the world view of the Kurdish leader

Abdullah Öcalan and in his ideas of freedom, justice and democracy. He quit his studies and went to the Kurdish heartland on the fringes of Turkey, Syria and Iraq. There he learned Kurmanji and found out how to use arms. From Marc the left wing idealist emerged Cihan Kendal the self-styled freedom fighter. That was in 2013.

Cihan Kendal and his band of seven men whose faces, weathered by sun and wind and the rigours of war, still shone with youth, were holed up on the edge of Ain Issa, a mere fifty kilometres from Raqqa, the biggest prize in the campaign against the black flag of IS. Once Raqqa fell the Islamic State would be vanquished. Since taking over Ain Issa and surrounding villages the previous June their platoon had engaged in constant skirmishes with IS. Hardly a day went by without IS attacking some Kurdish outpost. "They have more of everything than we do: guns, ammo, rocket throwers, tanks. We have to harbour our resources while they can afford to be reckless," said Cihan Kendal.

In the afternoon the man who had turned his back on Germany to start a world revolution was standing behind a wall of sandbags on the roof of his outpost, training his binoculars on the enemy position, an olive grove one kilometre away. Cihan Kendal passed a hand over his shaven skull and took a puff on his cigarette. All around was a vast, flat nothingness, a dry desert dominated by a grain silo like a medieval tower. An empty road crossed the scene and led straight to Raqqa, capital of the grim realm of Abu Bakr al-Bagdadi, self-anointed caliph of the so-called Islamic State. Cihan Kendal's eyes roved around, then settled on a couple of abandoned farmhouses where he thought IS fighters had dug in. He appraised the mud wall surrounding the post like a rampart and watched a mechanical digger fifty metres away making a trench separating free Syria from the IS domain. "Make it deeper and wider!" he shouted to the driver. "A little child could hop over that!"

It didn't take long for the IS spotters to notice the digger working out in the open. A puff of white smoke shot up from the olive grove, then there was a humming noise which rapidly grew louder. "Katyushka! Katyushka!" cried Kendal's men, giggling like schoolboys as they took cover behind the sandbags and in the stair well of the building, as if it was all a game. The first rocket landed a few metres to the left of the post; the second hit the building, sending bits of brick and shrapnel spinning in the air; the third flashed overhead and exploded in an empty field behind. "There they are, in the building next to the olive grove," shouted Kendal. His men fired. After peppering the IS hideout they slapped each other on the back and laughed. Cihan Kendal issued orders: inform US air command; provide coordinates; position anti-aircraft guns.

While the battle went on outside Cihan Kendal and his comrades sat in their bunker drinking tea and smoking cigarettes. "My lifestyle and priorities have altered, obviously," said Kendal, drawing the cigarette smoke deep into his lungs, "but I don't miss much, only my music. Bob Marley and Jimmy Cliff. No, I'm really happy here." He glanced at his comrades. Somewhere in the distance US jets were carrying out an air raid. Kendal admitted he felt bad about leaving his mother and younger brother without telling them where he was going or when he would return. He knew how they'd feel if they heard he'd fallen foul of IS. He hadn't been able to communicate with them for weeks. "It's hard for my mother to accept that I'm here. Naturally she worries. Still, she supports me in my decision. What riles me is the aggro she gets from some of her neighbours. Not everyone there approves of what I'm doing. Still, never mind." Just then a radio message came through: in a different sector a suicide bomber had driven a van towards a Kurdish post with the evident intention of destroying it, but the vehicle had exploded before getting there.

After their rocket attack the IS had withdrawn. Now USAF bombers and drones were circling high overhead. Cihan Kendal left his bunker, craned his head back and looked into the cloudless sky. "See, *heval*, our Kurdish air force!" he quipped, laughing loudly.

The following morning saw Cihan Kendal walking with one of his comrades along a path near his outpost as the mist dissolved in the morning sunshine. He was looking out for signs of recent digging or any unfamiliar object. All he found was an unexploded mortar shell. This check was a daily routine, as IS fighters were known to sometimes creep close to Kurdish positions under cover of darkness and place mines or booby traps on roads and paths.

My visit gave Cihan Kendal a break from the monotony and a chance to give a tour of the front. At another Kurdish outpost five kilometres from his we met a girl fighter kneeling on a rampart and surveying the neighbourhood with field glasses. She beckoned to Cihan Kendal. "Look, *heval*," she said, giving him the binoculars. About eight hundred metres away thirty or forty IS soldiers were loitering among the bushes and olive trees. "They're up to something," he hissed. He immediately set off, heading back to his own post in case an attack was imminent. On the way we came to a road sign saying 'Raqqa 50 km'. He asked the driver to stop, got out, pulled a felt pen from his pocket and wrote on the signboard the name he'd been known by in his leftist demonstration days, Zohan. The name may have come from a German TV comedy show featuring a spy called Zohan. Old habit had suddenly taken hold of him. He looked at the inscription and laughed. "Hamburg urban culture fifty kilometres from Raqqa," he said, shaking his head. A crazy world, Cihan Kendal's world.

The day after I left Syria IS fighters seized the Tishrin outpost where I had stayed for two days, killing six of the Kurdish fighters I shared a room with. On the way out of the country I passed Tel Abyad, which was supposed to be safely in Kurdish hands. The following morning IS attacked it and dozens of fighters died on either side.

I thought back over the past four years. I remembered the eve of the battle for Aleppo, when nobody yet imagined what horrors lay ahead for the city and its people and I, like most others, thought the war would be over within weeks.

Four years on, Aleppo was blockaded. The once proud city had turned into a sea of ruins. Such inhabitants as remained were prisoners in their own town. Of the activists who had welcomed me in 2012 all were dead, missing or in exile. Syria was a nightmare with no end.

I had visited Syria until it became too dangerous for foreign reporters to access the war zone. Too many of us had been kidnapped and murdered. Nevertheless, up until then I had managed to keep on with my work, observing the slow death of a city.

And now? Assad's barrel bombs and Putin's rockets were turning village after village, town after town to ashes. IS tyrants and hostile opposition factions, al-Qaida, people traders and antique robbers had descended on the city like a Biblical plague. World heritage sites like the Souq and the Umayyid Mosque lay in ruins, the proud citadel was damaged. Four hundred thousand people were dead, many more were wounded, millions had fled the country.

Hardly any of the people I had known in Syria, people who had befriended me, people who had shared their stories with me, people who had risked their lives for me, hardly any of them were still alive unless they had fled. The ones who escaped were now in Germany, Turkey or Lebanon – like Khaled of the White Helmets, Yosef my faithful Aleppo guide, Nermin the plucky editor. Omar, the brave photographer, was sitting the war out in a house with no furniture in Lebanon. Dr Othman, the despairing consultant from Aleppo, was living in Saarbrücken badly traumatized.

In spring 2016 I talked to my old friend Abu Yazan who was still obstinately refusing to leave his home in Aleppo. He was too proud to abandon his principles and become a refugee, preferring to die in Syria a free man. I failed in all my efforts to persuade him to flee; at least to send his family to Germany. We talked over Skype. An armistice had just come into force – and was holding, against all expectations. His son Mustafa had been seriously wounded in an artillery attack and had spent weeks in hospital. His eldest son Mohammed had been shot in the chest and it was a miracle he had survived. Abu Yazan told me how amazing it felt to be standing in the street outside his house and hear no explosions and no planes. "It's quite uncanny," he said.

That brief truce had long since ended. By dint of endless bombardment, the Syrian army and its allies – the Iranians, the Afghan conscripts and Hezbollah – with air support from Russia had succeeded in cutting off the only remaining supply route from Turkey into Aleppo. The city was cut off for twenty-five days; no medicines, diesel fuel or food could be brought in and none of the wounded could be taken out. The city was faced with starvation. Then a coalition of rebel bands mounted a desperate assault and broke through the siege.

Anyone who wished to contact people in Aleppo and find out what was going on there had to resort to Facebook, WhatsApp or Skype on shaky internet connections. In August 2016 I was talking to Dr Hamza Alkateab who was at Al-Quds Hospital in the city. Our connection was repeatedly interrupted and finally severed. Via WhatsApp the doctor asked me to put my questions in writing. Two days later I got the answers by voicemail. Dr Alkateab, a plumpish young man with slicked back hair and spectacles, outlined the daily horrors in a calm tone as if he had been a clerk in an office. He even apologized for his late reply. His eight-month old daughter was crying in the background.

Not a day was passing without attacks, more than forty per day. In the time it took him to reply to my questions he counted sixteen explosions. The regime was now using more cluster bombs than barrel bombs. Planes were circling over Aleppo without cease.

The few remaining hospitals received relief supplies and medicines once every three months. That was enough to treat the more urgent cases. "But we have only twelve doctors in our hospital and often get a hundred to a hundred and twenty wounded coming to us in a single day. We aren't able to treat everyone. Our ambulances are fired on and we are liable to be attacked any time."

For hospitals and clinics have become a target for Syrian and Russian air raids. So far, Al-Quds Hospital had been bombed three times. The time before last, on 27th April, a doctor, two nurses and a guard were killed. Five days ago another nurse had been killed in an attack. On 10th August the government troops had used chlorine gas and fifty-seven gas victims had to be treated.

Asked what the West could do to help the people of Aleppo the doctor laughed. After five years of war almost nobody in Aleppo still believed help would come. "We aren't terrorists, we're not IS, we don't cut people's heads off. We are Syrians who die to save our honour. We need a no-fly zone to stop civilians being massacred," said Alkateab, who knew no such thing would happen. His voice was weary. "The Syrian government's assertion that there are four corridors for civilians to leave the city is false. When people try to flee they are shot by snipers before they reach a corridor."

Naturally he feared death, and he worried for his wife and small daughter, too. "But it's my duty to stay and help my countrymen, too many doctors have already fled." Dr Hamza Alkateab had supported the revolution from the start and had demonstrated against the regime as early as 2011. "Since then hundreds of thousands have lost their lives, too many for the United Nations to count. Thousands of mothers have lost their sons, thousands of children have lost their parents. We must not allow that blood to have been shed in vain. That's why I stay on and stand against the regime." At that point he wished me goodbye, saying he was needed in the hospital.

In September 2016 Syria was back in the headlines: "Aleppo Under Siege", "Doctors and Hospitals Attacked", "War against IS". Meanwhile the foreign ministers of Russia and the USA strove to find a solution that would save face for both their countries; Syria's own interests were of course a minor issue. Some media interest was revived, after years when Syria's daily suffering had been met with indifference and the excuse of "non-interference" had been reiterated like a mantra. The time for a political or military solution seemed long past; the West had given up. Each proudly heralded truce soon collapsed and gave way to renewed bombing. There was a shocking indifference to the horror faced by the people of Aleppo and other Syrian cities. The images of citizens buried under ruins, children torn apart by bombs, slaughtered doctors and starving townsfolk ceased to affect those who saw them. The world seemed to have become accustomed to such horror, and also to the idea that there was nothing anyone could do to stop the killing.

I wondered how the tragedy of Syria might have played out if the West had given more (or different) support to the moderate indigenous opposition elements before extremists had a chance to move in and hijack the revolution. What might a no-fly zone have achieved? Or a safe corridor for civilians? What if the red lines drawn by the USA, but later shifted and ignored by Assad, had been backed up with genuine and sincere sanctions? I am no supporter of intervention; I demonstrated against the invasion of Afghanistan, and I believe that the invasion of Iraq, instead of extinguishing a small bonfire in the Middle East, started a huge conflagration. First Bush rode rough-shod over the principle of national sovereignty to occupy Iraq; later Obama ordered a hasty withdrawal of American troops; each of those moves was harmful. Of course without the first the second would not have happened.

Probably the war would have been long over if the West had got actively involved instead of just watching from the side-lines, relying on shady allies. By side-stepping the issue, it facilitated the chaotic developments it wished to avoid and the Islamic State seized its chance to spread throughout Syria. The refugee crisis, too, would never have become so huge that it threatened the balance of Europe. Most Syrians had endured three hard years in Syria or in grim refugee camps in Jordan, Turkey and Lebanon in the hope that the war would soon end; only after the last spark of hope had died did so many knock on Europe's doors. Then suddenly, Syria's problems no longer seemed so distant, they affected people in Europe. That was the result of earlier inaction; if something had been done in time the refugee crisis, the rise of the extreme right and the Brexit fiasco would never have come to pass.

I knew there would be no end to the fighting in Syria, let alone lasting peace, as long as Assad remained in power. The war had acquired a momentum of its own, Syria had become a political football in a power game with several different players each with their own ends, and there could be no real winner. The Islamic State was rapidly losing ground in one defeat after another. The Kurds, at considerable cost, had taken over the IS stronghold of Manbij. Then the Turks had sent tanks into Syria ostensibly to fight the IS, thus adding to the foreign presence in the country. With the help of Syrian rebel militias, they had indeed taken Jarablous from the IS within a matter of hours; but that was incidental to their real aim of repelling the Kurds and preventing them from establishing their own state. Now Turks were fighting Kurds on Syrian soil; opening up yet another war front.

It was almost impossible to make sense of the turmoil in Syria. Assad and Russia were together fighting both USA-supported rebels and IS troops; in Aleppo Syrian chlorine bombs and Russian firebombs were falling. Kurds hitherto supported by the USA felt betrayed when Turkey, a NATO ally of the United States, turned its guns on them with American blessings. Different factions vied with each other: Kurds against Arabs, Arabs against Kurds, Arabs against Arabs, Shiites and Alawis against Sunnis, and all of them against IS. It was impossible to disentangle such a web or predict what lay ahead.

In Iraq, too, IS dominance was coming to an end, but the next round of conflict could be foreseen: Kurds fighting the Iraqi army which was vying for control of the areas the Kurds had won back from IS; Sunnis fighting Shiites. A majority of Sunnis viewed the IS as the lesser of two evils since they did protect Sunnis from Shiite death squads. There would only be peace in Iraq when the two main sects of Islam stopped fighting each other.

In summer 2016, at a beer garden in Munich, I met Ahmad and Hanadi, the severely burned brother and sister from Homs whose lives we had saved. We hugged in silence for minutes, then sat together under a chestnut tree. I was drinking beer while they had blackcurrant smoothies. Ahmad had the long black locks of a rock star and by now his German was almost accent free. Hanadi's face still had scars from the fateful day when Syrian shells had exploded in the family kitchen in Homs. She had difficulty speaking because her thorax had been burned. Now a young lady 17 years old, she wavered between self-possession and embarrassment, often having to hide her face in her headscarf. I knew she posted pictures of her new life in Germany on Facebook, but blocked out her own face with smiley emoticons. She intended to get her school leaving certificate and then go on to study at university. Ahmed had begun training as a medico-technical assistant. "Without the help of German doctors neither my sister nor I would have survived, so now I want to help others," he explained. Their parents were still living in a refugee camp in Lebanon and they hadn't seen them since 2012; Facebook, Skype and WhatsApp were their only link to their land of origin. "Germany is now our home country," they said, full of pride and gratitude.

Chapter 18: Return to Sinjar, March 2017

I had been writing about the fate of the Yazidi people since the days ISIS overran the Yazidi settlements in northern Iraq in 2014. The future of this religious minority was being decided in their spiritual and cultural heartland, the Sinjar mountains in northern Iraq. The IS had been driven out. Mosul, a once proud Biblical town, had been destroyed in the bombardments carried out by its liberators.

In March 2017 I returned to the region to seek answers to the question, what future do the Yazidis now have in Iraq? It was a very sobering experience.

Just getting to Sinjar was a feat of logistics. The areas liberated from IS control could only be visited with the permission of the Kurdish autonomous authorities plus a visa from the Iraqi government. Vehicles ran up against dozens of checkpoints where grumpy guards suspiciously checked passports and visas. The journey was a long and dangerous one, skirting the battlefields of previous years: from the Kurdish metropolis of Erbil, over the Tigris, through bomb-blasted Mosul, over damaged bridges, past the grave of Jonah and the ruined al-Nuri mosque, to Tal Afar, the town out of which IS had just been driven. Sleeper cells of IS were still active there, killing sentries, kidnapping Shiites and Kurds. After Tal Afar an empty road led through deserted no man's land beside the Syrian border. Abandoned villages and ruined houses flashed past the window. After a four hour drive the bulk of a table-mountain rose out of the haze on the horizon. At the foot of the northern side of Mount Sinjar lay the town of the same name. Forty thousand people had once lived in it, but now it was a ghost town to which life was only just returning.

In August 2014 images of desperate Yazidis fleeing up Mount Sinjar in panic from the approaching IS troops were seen on television screens all over the world. Sinjar was liberated in November 2015. I was the only Western reporter in town to witness the liberation. The Kurdish and Yazidi fighters who sacrificed so much had high hopes that things would change for them. They were wrong. Two and a half years after the IS reign of terror Sinjar was still in ruins. The first thing I did in Sinjar was visiting a school.

The teacher was sitting in front of a mountain of papers he despaired of reducing. Take a sheet from the pile, signature here, rubber stamp there, next sheet. From time to time he wiped his hand on his trousers or massaged his fingers which ached from writing. It was the first day of term. The air was thick in the yellow painted teachers' common room at Almukhtalad public school in Sinjar. Interim reports for 1200 pupils had to be prepared, and he with some voluntary assistants had been working at them for hours. The assistants were young people full of enthusiasm: young men in pipe jeans and undercuts, smart girls with lacquered fingernails and no headscarves. These small details of appearance signified rejection of the oppressive rules once imposed by the IS. These thirty-two helpers had come back from the refugee camps to help rebuild their town. They were thankful to have something to do at last, as the teacher explained. Khero Qaso Wahab, 52, was a friendly man with snow white hair, a silver moustache and kindly eyes. He apologized for having to keep working during the interview as he was under pressure. He was a unique figure in the war-battered town, for he was Sinjar's only salaried teacher. "I teach the hundred and four students in the sixth," he explained, wiping sweat from his brow. "The other classes are taught by my assistants."

Mr Wahab had to teach whatever was required: Arabic, history, maths, geography. He also had to stand in whenever one of the helpers was absent. For his pains he received 700 dollars a month from the Iraqi government. He had been a teacher for twenty-seven years, but the job had never been as difficult as it was now. "We haven't got enough books or tables or chairs. We haven't yet established a timetable. The school reopened last October after being closed for three years. Some of our pupils had been abducted, some lost their parents. They're afraid in case *Da'ish* comes back again. They cry a lot and can't concentrate." *Da'ish*, that terrifying word, the Arabic acronym for Islamic State. IS had been defeated but memories of its terrible actions still afflicted the inhabitants of Sinjar like a curse. For Khero Qaso Wahab, like almost everyone in the school, was a Yazidi.

Of all religious groups the Yazidis stood top in the IS hit list. The Yazidi community is an ancient, closed and secretive faith group of which one can only become a member by birth. No outsider can convert to the Yazidi faith or join the community by marriage. Sunni extremists view Yazidis as devil worshippers – an error, as there is no devil in the Yazidi belief system, which is monotheistic and emerged in Mesopotamia about five thousand years ago. It has no prophet and no holy book. The object of worship is an almighty creator composed of light whose name is Taus-i-Melek or peacock angel. Remarkably, in Yazidi belief there is good but not evil. An irony of history is that in spite of that the Yazidis have always been persecuted: the campaign against them carried out by IS ranked as the seventy-fourth genocide in their history.

The history of the Yazidis over the centuries reads like a buccaneer novel. First came the invasion of Mesopotamia by the Arabs in the 7th century. Already by that time Mount Sinjar had become a place of refuge for persecuted Yazidis. Next came the Mongol hordes in the 13th century. In the 17th century it was the Othman who tried to pick out the Yazidi people.

As ever the mountain offered protection from marauding armies, like an impregnable natural fortress. It was not until after the Gulf War of 1991 that the Yazidis were promised specific rights within an autonomous Kurdish region: they were empowered to set up schools, pass on their cultural heritage, practise their beliefs freely. In August 2014 the IS legions of death descended on the Yazidis like a Biblical plague, killing, abducting and raping thousand upon thousand. It was an event so frightful its shock waves would be felt far into the future.

Now, after so much genocide and persecution, some eight hundred thousand Yazidis exist worldwide. 650,000 are in Iraq and the largest group in the diaspora, about 120,000 people, are settled in Germany. Tens of thousands are to be found in Russia, Syria, Georgia and Armenia.

Iraq is the historical and religious homeland of the Yazidis. Many scholars think that the Kurds were originally Yazidis only they later converted to Islam. Nowadays Yazidis often wish their ancestors had chosen somewhere else to live other than the land between the Tigris and Euphrates rivers which has been so prone to war, hatred, corruption and religious zealotry. It is a perpetual crisis zone where, since the withdrawal of the American occupation forces in 2011, different religious and ethnic groups have been grating against each other like tectonic plates before an earthquake. Shiites are pitted against

Sunnis, Sunnis and Shiites against Kurds, each against each in turn. Most recently Shiites, Sunnis and Kurds did join together to eject the IS, half ruining the country in the process. Hardly had IS been beaten when Kurdish calls for independence threatened to unleash a civil war. The Yazidis had to sit tight in the midst of this political and religious turmoil.

How tight they were sitting could be judged by considering three places in the Yazidi heartlands around Sinjar in northern Iraq. First, a small pilgrimage town where a Yazidi general was feeling hemmed in by enemies. Second, the ruined town of Sinjar itself, on the northern flank of Mount Sinjar, where nearly three years after the expulsion of IS an element of normality was beginning to return. Third, a refugee camp on the top of the table-mountain where 13,000 refugees were still living in a tent city having lost all hope of a decent future.

On a cold February morning one thousand two hundred girls and boys set out from their homes among the ruins of the town, hungry for knowledge. Arriving at the iron gate of the school they greeted the friendly janitor and crowded into their classrooms as if eager to make up for lost time. Their head teacher Khero Qaso Wahab, mindful that they had all been through dreadful times, greeted them warmly. He knew that attending his school was helping them regain their confidence and high spirits. He handed his bundle of school reports to a young assistant and led his visitor upstairs to the second floor, patting a couple of boys on the head as he passed along a sun-filled corridor. He stopped at a classroom door, knocked and entered.

As he entered the room sixty-two sixth form pupils jumped up from their chairs and chorused, "Good morning, teacher." The children, the nation's future, were squeezed two to a chair and four to a desk. In front of the class a young man with rimless spectacles was standing by the blackboard. He was wearing a black jacket, black jeans and sneakers. Today Arabic grammar was on Jassim Murad's teaching plan. Mr Wahab politely asked him if he might interrupt for a moment, as he wanted to ask the children a few questions for the benefit of his foreign visitor. The young teacher gave a slight bow to show he assented to his senior colleague's request.

"Which of you missed school for more than a year?" asked Khero Qaso Wahab. Twenty-five hands shot up. Eleven pupils had missed two years, four had missed three.
"Which of you lost family members to IS?" Nineteen boys jumped up. 12-year old Amram's father and uncle had been beheaded by the IS. Twelve members of 15-year old Haydar's family were still missing. 13-year old Ziad had watched his grandmother being shot dead.

"Who was responsible for those things?"

"The Arabs!" cried all sixty-two boys.

When the older teacher asked what should be done with the perpetrators the boys replied in one voice that all Arabs should be killed. Asked what they hoped to do when they grew up they named professions such as teacher, doctor, engineer, pilot, policeman. One hoped to be a footballer. Which thing did they want most of all? Revenge, they cried in unison. This was followed by a brief silence, then a ripple of nervous laughter as if someone had just cracked a tasteless joke.

Khero Qaso Wahab left the classroom with drooping shoulders as if an invisible burden was pressing down on him. "I've almost given up hope for Iraq," he sighed. Correcting himself, he added immediately that there was hope still, or rather hope once again. On his way down the stairs Mr Wahab suddenly stopped as if he had thought of something. He glanced at his watch; the time was 3:40 p.m. "Classes won't be over for another twenty minutes, time to show you something that would have been unimaginable a while ago." He opened the door of a different classroom, revealing a raft of desks jammed together and behind them fourteen children whose dress suggested they were Muslims. The girls were all wearing headscarves. By the blackboard in front of the class stood the Islamic studies teacher Miss Hadir

Yahya, 21, the only Shiite member of staff. She adjusted her headscarf in embarrassment when Mr Wahab came in. He apologized for disturbing her and asked her to carry on teaching. "This is the first and only class for Shiite children in Sinjar," he whispered to his visitor. "These are our children too. We must help them to get educated." He sounded proud. The fact that some Shiites were returning to Sinjar was a good sign, he said, it was evidence of fellow feeling – for IS had persecuted the Shiites almost as much as the Yazidis.

School ended punctually at 4 p.m. The twelve hundred pupils poured out of Almukhtalad Comprehensive School chattering and laughing, politely greeting members of staff and saying goodbye to the janitor who waved at them smiling. Some boys played football in the dust, using an empty can as their ball. Khero Qaso Wahab proudly watched them go, then set out for his own home which was a fifteen-minute walk from the school. He said he was glad that life was gradually returning to his home town, even if it could never again be like it used to be. He pointed out a couple of shops with bananas, tomatoes and potatoes on display. Other signs of life were all around. A few small supermarkets among the ruins had telephone cards, soft drinks and cigarettes for sale. The smell of freshly baked bread came from a baker's shop. A man with a huge moustache was serving two soldiers at his kebab stall. Some youths in Real Madrid and Barcelona shirts were playing football in an open square. A wedding party drove through the streets with horns blaring. Sinjar had begun to slough off its memories of horror layer by layer, as a snake sheds its skin.

It was no easy task, for there were numerous reminders of the IS reign of terror, burned out houses, ruined temples, mass graves. Mr Wahab pointed out the Arabic letters spray-painted on the doors of buildings: For Sunni, for Shiite, for Yazidi, that sort of thing. "Our Arab neighbours did that," he said. "They betrayed us to the *Da'ish*."

Mr Wahab's reopening of the school constituted a ray of hope and a triumph over the IS bigots who had condemned books, education, music and every kind of amusement. Other men had been making positive moves in the political field. One of them was Murat Khalaf el-Khaleti, a handsome strongly built man in his early thirties, who could be seen making his way through the ruined streets of the old quarter of Sinjar dressed in a black suit and polished leather shoes. He had been born and brought up in Sinjar. For fifteen months, with other Yazidis, he had fought alongside PKK against IS in the narrow alleys of the old town. I had met him years before in the trenches and ruins of his city. When at last the terrorists had been driven out he had hung up his

Kalashnikov and turned politician. He felt sick of war and death and thought it was time to secure the future of the Yazidis and rebuild the town so the refugees could return home. With fellow veterans he founded the Yazidi Party for Freedom and Democracy or PADE, of which he became Vice President. The party was politically close to PKK and its goal was to create a self-governing Sinjar independent from both Kurdistan and Iraq. "We're tired of being second class citizens."

The eerie silence in Sinjar meant there was a lot of work to do. Murat stopped, put his hand to his ear and listened. Not a sound was to be heard. He kicked an empty shell case aside and climbed up a mound of rubble that had once been someone's home. He clambered through the ruins to see shattered crockery, a battered teapot, an orphaned doll. "Nobody is helping or doing anything for us," he complained. "Why is that? Because we are Yazidis. Mosul is being rebuilt all right, but here nothing has been done." He covered his nose with a handkerchief as a stench of rotting flesh wafted from a house, for bodies were still lying under the rubble. As he stepped back a young woman in the uniform of the Yazidi Defence Brigades came running towards him waving her arms. "Landmines!" she cried. She stopped in front of Murat, panting for breath, and told him it was too dangerous for civilians to walk there. Murat thanked her politely for the warning. "It's incredible, the town hasn't yet been cleared of mines," he muttered to himself, brushing dust from his suit.

While Murat Khalaf el-Khaleti was walking through Sinjar's ruins he listed the things which were wrong and ran out of fingers to keep tally. "No electricity, no water, no garbage collection, no paid employment, mines everywhere... no wonder people aren't returning." For once the smile had vanished from the face of this mild, amiable man and his words were bitter. He took a deep breath to calm himself. I asked him what future he thought Sinjar had. "I don't like using the word future, it goes with false promises and false hopes. But I became a politician to make things better."

In May parliamentary elections were going to take place in Iraq, with 328 assembly seats to be contested. PADE was entering the race, for as Murat said, only through political process could the Yazidis' condition be improved, and for that they needed to have representatives in parliament. The former freedom fighter spoke out frankly, smoking one cigarette after another and ignoring the mobile phone which kept ringing in his pocket. He knew a long road lay ahead for his party. "Unfortunately we haven't all got exactly the same goals, but still we're all Yazidis," he said.

When Sinjar had been liberated instead of a consensus plan emerging for the future of all Yazidis there had been argument and strife. Different groups had staked out their own claims with flags in different parts of the town. There was the yellow flag of the Kurdish PDK, the red and green flag of the religious Yazidis with Lalish temple on it, the yellow and green flag with stars belonging to the PKK and its ally the Yazidi Defence Brigades (YBS), and the white-red-white flag with a sun on it belonging to the Hêza Parastina Êzîdxan (HPE) or Yazidi Citizens' Army. At one stage the flag of Kurdistan with a rising sun on it had also fluttered everywhere. It was a real battle of flags which had begun with squabbles among the victors just hours after the final IS fighter had bitten the dust on 13th November 2015, the day of liberation. After the independence referendum the Kurdish flag had disappeared, but instead Iraqi and Shia flags had been seen flying over the town.

The situation had not got much better since then. Murat met two women searching for anything of value among the rubble in the old quarter: copper wire, iron rod, broken furniture which could be used as fuel. Their skin was sunburnt and cracked by cold, their hair was clotted with filth. When they spotted the politician they gave him a painful smile. A short conversation followed. The women explained how they had returned to Sinjar three months earlier. Their own home had been destroyed by bombing. "Now we're living in the house of an IS leader," said the elder of the two. The younger said they could consider it their own now, as the Arabs would not dare to come back.

Murat Khalaf el-Khaleti looked at the women for a moment, then gave them a handout of cash, 25,000 Iraqi dinar or about 15 dollars. He walked on for another two hundred metres, then stopped at a rusty barbed wire fence behind which the bones of thirty-two murdered Yazidis lay in a mass grave. "Members of my family are still missing," he said. "We don't know where they are or whether they're still alive. What future have we, you say? I often ask myself that question. My generation will never be really happy again, but maybe the next generation will be better off."

Back at PADE party Headquarters Murat served sweet tea and roast sunflower seeds. Party workers on their way in and out greeted him and exchanged hugs. Many had fought with him at the front. A young man came in to ask if his water cistern could be filled. Murat took his address and promised that a water lorry would call on him the next day. Then he got up to go: he was needed at a party meeting in Khansassor, a small town on the other side of the mountain. "It's about an irrigation system to let the peasants water their fields," he explained as his driver urged him to get moving.

Half way between Sinjar and Khansassor was the refugee camp of Serdashte. The road wound up Mount Sinjar like a corkscrew, reaching an altitude of 1463 metres. By the roadside lay burned vehicles and scraps of clothing from the bodies of Yazidis killed while trying to flee. Murat made a halt at the Yazidi martyrs' graveyard at Shebel Qasim, where next to a temple lay two hundred and eighty of the freedom fighters alongside whom he had fought. Bereaved kinswomen – mothers, wives, sisters – had left flowers and tresses of their hair on the graves. Murat had known each and every one of the dead. "No," he said at the grave of an uncle, "it won't be possible for us to live alongside the Arabs anymore."

Immediately after the graveyard the refugee camp of Serdashte began: six kilometres of misery on the Mount Sinjar plateau. For more than three years some two thousand families, thirteen to fourteen thousand human beings had been living in tents there. The area was extremely harsh and inhospitable even without any IS terrorists around. Midsummer temperatures reached fifty degrees Celsius, icy winds roared through in winter, and in the rainy season there were seas of mud.

"Still, we don't want to leave," said Ali Shabo Derwish. "Where could we go?" The 39-year old with his bald brow and stubbly chin was sitting cross-legged in his tent. He was surrounded by elderly men with white hair and long beards, all clan leaders and clerics, who nodded in agreement. Some were sipping sweet tea, some fingering prayer beads or smoking roll-ups. Ali Shabo Derwish was the nominal manager of Serdashte, in charge of the gloom. "We are second class citizens," he moaned. "Nobody does anything for us." A whisper went around the company, swiftly growing to a clamour. There are still mines in my house, said one. We have no doctors, no schools, no electricity, said another. A German NGO had provided generators but there was no diesel to run them. A pregnant woman had had to walk for hours to the nearest town to give birth, and then found the hospital closed because of staff shortages.

It seemed the people on the mountain top were trapped in a time warp where past, present and future were confused and merged. Up on top extremes of weather, hunger and misery. Down below mined and ruined houses. In between, a feeling of omnipresent enemies. People didn't know where to turn. Awful memories were too fresh, hatred and fear of a terrible oppressor were too great. "We only feel safe up here," said the camp manager. He would not reply to a question about the future of the Yazidis; instead he asked the visitor to get into his car.

He drove a couple of hundred metres through the camp, then turned left along a cart track, and after a couple of minutes stopped outside a tent near where some goats and donkeys were grazing in a meadow. A team of young men, smudged with soot, were busy making charcoal from branches.

In the semi-darkness of the tent Sherin Ferhan was sitting on the hard ground, her eyes red from weeping. Her six-year old son Delshad was wriggling in her lap: he was a puny child and he kept yelling and flailing his arms, only quieting down when allowed to play on his mother's smartphone. "He has a panic attack whenever he hears a plane. He can't sleep at night. He screams and lashes out," explained his mother. She was forty years old and a mother of eight. White hair spilled out from under her mauve head cloth and tears ran down her cheeks. Her voice kept faltering and she kept putting her hand on her chest and struggling for breath. It was only two weeks since the family had managed to pay the ransom for Delshad. For two and a half years the child had been in the hands of IS. Now he spoke only Arabic; he could recite many surah of the Quran by heart. But apparently he had also watched videos showing how to decapitate people.

The family had paid nearly twenty thousand dollars to his abductors, via a middleman. That included all their savings plus a similar amount borrowed from relatives and friends. The IS had kidnapped a total of four children from the family. One daughter had not survived; two children had been bought back; a final daughter was possibly still being held somewhere, though they didn't even know whether she was still alive.

While the bereft mother was telling her tale her son broke free from her and ran out of the tent. He started merrily throwing stones at Khalaf and Jamal, two neighbouring boys who suffered from polio. "We have no future, me and my children," said Sherin Ferhan, tucking a strand of hair back inside her headscarf. "I've become an old woman overnight. I can never be happy again. Sooner or later they'll kill the other kidnapped children, maybe they're already dead, I don't know. The only solution is to migrate, to Europe or Australia. Only then will we be safe." She added in a whisper that she would sooner die, but must not, because her children needed her.

Just then a donkey walked past the tent and Ali Shabo Derwish, the camp leader, observed that the situation might be less awful if all politicians were to be replaced by donkeys. For a moment there was general laughter. Then little Delshad reappeared and threw a stone at his mother.

Anyone looking for an answer to the question why, in spite of all the adversities, Yazidis still try to live in the Sinjar area needs to visit the pilgrim town of Sherfeddin, eleven kilometres as the crow flies from Sinjar town and nestling on the opposite side of the mountain.

One spring-like March morning four perspiring men were toiling over the hard limestone soil of the cemetery in Sherfeddin with spades and pickaxes. The sand-coloured steeple of the temple glowed in the morning sunshine. They hacked at the sun-baked earth for hours, digging centimetre by centimetre deeper into the ground. Local inhabitants gathered around the new grave, ready to take their leave from the deceased, 16-year old Mairam Husen, who had committed suicide in a refugee camp the night before. Women dressed in black sobbed over the girl's body, which was wrapped in a cloth, and slapped their cheeks in a ritualized show of grief. "Why have you left us with such pain? Haven't we suffered enough already?" A few steps away from the women mourners stood a young man with a tearstained face, his hands deep in his trouser pockets. It was the dead girl's brother-in-law, Raka. He told how Mairam had hanged herself in his father's tent, and his brother, her husband, had then been arrested for questioning to see if he was in any way connected with her suicide. His father would not come to the funeral as he had been against the marriage. Mairam was laid to rest beside her cousin Ali Hussein, killed eight months earlier by an IS landmine. She left a husband and a five-month old daughter. "She just couldn't stand this life any longer," said Raka resignedly; but at least she is buried in consecrated ground.

Sherfeddin is the second holiest place for Yazidis, after Lalish with its great temple. There in Sherfeddin a former landscape gardener from Westphalia in Germany, a hero of the recent war, was guarding the grave of a warrior who had resisted the Mongol invasion in the 13th century. General Kasim Shesho, by now 66 years of age, still a man of few words, with an even thicker moustache and a slightly balder forehead, was dressed in camouflaged battle fatigues and wore reflective sunglasses. He spoke with the gravelly voice of a chain smoker. His supporters called him the Lion of Sinjar or Lord of the Mountain and he was the guardian of the holy sites.

The previous few years had taught the Lion to be cautious. He frowned at the horizon where two Iraqi battle helicopters were firing rockets into a field. A child started to cry and the general's telephone was ringing. No, he said, he didn't know what was going on over there. He went up on the roof with his field glasses. Yes, he must get to the bottom of it straight away. No, he couldn't imagine that the Iraqi army would attack the Yazidis. A couple of telephone calls established that the provincial governor was on a visit to Sinjar and two bored helicopter pilots had decided to pass the time while waiting for him by doing a little shooting practice. There was no intention of frightening anyone.

When his people is uneasy, a leader has to show his face and reassure them to prevent chaos. General Shesho got his chauffeur to drive him through his realm and up onto a hillside. Rays of sunshine were breaking through the thick cloud cover. From up there he let his eyes rove over his shrunken domain, a barren stretch of land with a few trees and bushes. Below was the temple with its sand-coloured spires. "The bodies of sixty-five Yazidis murdered by *Da'ish* are buried right here," he said, pointing to the hard brown earth.

Shesho scraped the dust with his foot. There was no gravestone, no inscription, no monument to record the suffering of those people. There were dozens of such anonymous mass graves all over the mountain, with sun-bleached bones and skulls poking out of them. "It was the Sunnis who turned against us," growled the general, lighting a cigarette. "We won't let them come back. If they did return they would make another attempt to wipe us out." He surveyed the steep slopes and ravines of the Sinjar range, where he had fought Saddam Hussein's army as a young man. Enemies come and go in Iraq, but the mountains remain. "We revere this mountain," the general said. "Without it our people would not have survived." A crude message was still visible on the side of the mountain. It dated from the time when Sherfeddin was surrounded by IS troops. Some people had written "HELP US" on the hillside in giant letters using lumps of stone.

While Shesho walked through Sinjar he talked of his past. It was difficult to get details out of him as he was sparing with words; he raced through the story of his life like a speeded-up film. He told of imprisonment and torture under Saddam Hussein, of a sentence to death which had been transmuted to life imprisonment and finally annulled. After his release from prison he had fled with his family, first to Syria, then in the early 1990s to Germany where he obtained political asylum and took German citizenship. For twenty-four years he had alternated between being a landscape gardener in Bad Oeynhausen and a revered celebrity in the Sinjar mountains. His sons and daughters matriculated from school, studied at university, did their military service, got jobs, started families; it was an orderly and unremarkable kind of life, and he had thought his soldier days were behind him. Then *Da'ish* had overrun his homeland. "Germany was kind to me and my family. But Sinjar is my home, and I was needed here."

For two years Shesho defended Sherfeddin with a couple of hundred comrades. He served as leader of an alliance of Kurdish and Yazidi militias, which eventually, in November 2015, drove IS out of the Sinjar region. At the peak of his power as commander he was in control of all the villages in the sixty-kilometre-long mountain range and had nine thousand fighters under him, equipped and paid by the Kurdish autonomous authority under president Masud Barzani. Yet this general with his huge moustache came out the biggest loser in the political turmoil which overtook Sinjar after the fall of the Islamic caliphate.

For in September 2017, in a fit of excessive hubris fed by the euphoria of victory, ignoring the advice of his allies and heedless of Iraqi government warnings, Barzani declared independence for Kurdistan. The Iraqi government immediately deployed its army to subdue the insubordinate Kurds, and within weeks the Kurds lost a third of their territory including the oilfields of Kirkuk and the region of Sinjar. They had ground to a halt. Kasim Shesho had fought alongside them, but now he and his followers withdrew to Sherfeddin. "It's like August 2014 all over again. We're hemmed in all round by an enemy," he observed.

Nevertheless, he said, he would not act any differently another time. Loyalty was essential to survival in that barren region. Barzanis Peshmerga had been the only ones who stood by the Yazidis when it came to the crunch, in good times or bad.

The general sat down with his comrades in arms, old fellows with long beards who had fought over and again throughout their lives and were now passing on their skills to a new generation. Each evening before retiring to his quarters Kasim Shesho liked to mix with his men and play cards, stand a round of beer, crack jokes, say words of encouragement.

By now the Islamic State was just one more dark chapter in Yazidi history, said Shesho. What would come next was anybody's guess. He thought the long term future of the Yazidis lay in an independent Kurdistan. In the short term it was just a matter of defending the holy sites from possible enemies. He shrugged his shoulders: that was how matters stood. Only one thing was certain: "Whatever happens, we're going to stay put. This is our motherland, our holy sites are here, our forefathers are all buried here. This is where we will defend our people and our faith."

A long day was drawing to a close. Kasim Shesho lit a cigarette and blew smoke into the purple evening sky. Twenty-two perspiring young men were battling it out on the volleyball court he had created next to the assembly hall of the pilgrim centre, whamming the ball to and fro over the net. Seeing their commander in chief walk past they called out to him. *"Hol hol'a Taus-i-Melek'a! Hol hol'a Sherfeddin'a!"* they cried. It was the battle cry of the Yazidis of Sherfeddin. A smile appeared under the general's mighty moustache. He was on his way to the temple, for every Thursday and Friday Yazidis go to the Sherfeddin shrine to say their prayers. Flanked by his bodyguard the general led the way, closely followed by his son Yassir, his officers and a cluster of others.

Dusk was already falling as the general entered the temple. The men took off their shoes and walked across the polished marble tiles in their socks. Kasim Shesho kissed the sacred walls of the temple, sat cross-legged on the floor and with his eyes closed prayed for the future of his people while a priest fanned the flames in a censer. Then everyone gave thanks to Taus-i-Melek, the angel made of light who has the form of a peacock. It seemed the men found their moment of peace in this inner sanctum of the Yazidi temple, enclosed by thick walls dating from the 13th century, and forgot for a while what the zealots of the Islamic State had done to them and their people.

The general and his entourage fanned the smoke from the holy flames into their faces and for a minute their features relaxed. Nobody spoke. Even the general's bodyguard closed their eyes and let their rifles sink to the ground while their lips moved silently in prayer. It was a fleeting moment of peace, sustained by the hope that it would endure longer than the smoke from the sacred fire.

Acknowledgements

My special thanks go to my wife who lets me run away yet always allows me back into her arms.

This book could not have come into being without the help of various people. Thanks to Frank Brunner who tirelessly goes through my writings and suggests improvements. I could not have done this book without his help. Thanks to everyone at the Zeitenspiegel agency, who support me without demur and enable me to carry on my work in accordance with my ethical and moral principles: Uli Reinhardt, Tilman Wörtz, Uschi Entenmann, Erdmann Wingert, Philipp Mausshardt, Jan Rübel, Edeltraud Schneider, Wolfgang Dising. Thanks to the people who remain my friends in spite of being far away: Marcel Mettelsiefen, Alexander Bühler, Tina Günder, Dr. Susanne Kadner, Sofia Mpalampanis, Andrea Mühlthaler, Kristina Moreno, Dominik Schiess, Verena Fiebiger, Oliver Fritz, Dr Eba Pasha, Tarik Abdin-Bey, Ahmad und Hanadi Abbas, Armin Smailovic, Veronika Faltenbacher, Marc Deininger, David Eubank, Guy Calaf, Phelim Kyne, Melissa Stewart, Carlo Gabuco, Patricia Evangelista, Veejay Villafranca, Gordon Kricke, Michael und Anjana Hasper.

Thanks to the Editorial Board of *Der Spiegel*, to Amnesty International, Cicero, NZZ on Sunday,

Bastei Lübbe, *Weltspiegel*, *Auslandsjournal* und Spiegel TV, who offer a platform for my work.

Without the support and help of many people it would not have been possible for me to carry out my enquiries in Syria and Iraq: Thanks to Abdullah Ibrahim for his fraternal kindness, to Ruham Hawash, Fadi Aloush, Omar Zabadani, Miriam Zabadani, Nivin Dalati, Josef Abubaker, Hassan Ashwor, the White Helmets team, Yassir al-Haj, Majad Radwan, Agir.

Last but not least I must thank "Uncle" Roger Gwynn and my old friend Jaya Black for painstakingly translating my writings.

I must beg the forgiveness of my family, for living at the opposite end of the world and for all the fears and worries they endure on my account: my mother Rita Stormer, my sister Katja Rehnig and her husband Steffen Rehnig, Gerda Pein, Andreas Stormer, Mechthild Stormer. I miss you all.

And I wish to place on record my fond memory and gratitude to the many friends and helpers who did not survive those terrible wars.

www.ingramcontent.com/pod-product-compliance
Lightning Source LLC
Chambersburg PA
CBHW031053250726
48655CB00004B/1420